A Two-Dollar Bet Means Murder

A Two-Dollar Bet Means Murder

by

FRED J. COOK

1961

THE DIAL PRESS NEW YORK

Library of Congress Catalog Card Number: 61-7366

This book is based on material that appeared in *The Nation*, October 22, 1960, under the title "Gambling, Inc."

Second Printing, June 1961

DESIGNED BY WILLIAM R. MEINHARDT
PRINTED IN THE UNITED STATES OF AMERICA
BY THE HADDON CRAFTSMEN, SCRANTON, PA.

CONTENTS

A Two-Dollar Bet Means Murder

1

RULE OF THE LAWLESS

THE wife of a wage earner in Syracuse, New York, was desperate. Her husband earned some $7,000 a year, but his family was nearly destitute. They were three payments in arrears on a large furniture bill; their clothes were shabby, their food scant; their gas and electricity were about to be shut off. This impoverishment in the midst of adequate income was caused by just one factor; the husband was a victim of a psychological disease worse in some ways than the affliction of the alcoholic—he was possessed by an insatiable urge to gamble.

Within the past year and a half, he had gone back time and again to the gambling game being run wide open in Syracuse by "big-shot" gamblers. The game was no secret. The boss gambler had been doing business at the same spot for twenty-five years. Tapped on the wrist just four times by minor fines, he had conducted a lawless business in full view of the law, almost as openly as a businessman runs a department store. The $7,000-a-year wage earner was simply one of innumerable victims.

This fact did not, of course, mitigate his personal tragedy. Hooked by losses, the wage earner kept going back to get even. With the blind, unreasoning, total commitment of the addict, he kept seeking the big killing that would wipe out all his losses. Inevitably, he always wound up fleeced of his last available dollar and owing the house. In terror then—for he was playing with gamblers whom one did not continue to owe with impunity—he scrabbled for money. He borrowed his working wife's last cent; he got loans from the banks, from a credit union. In eighteen months the $7,000-a-year wage earner had lost $8,000.

"I called the police on one occasion about my husband's gambling, and a detective told me it was difficult to make gambling arrests and apparently there was little they could do," the distraught wife wrote in a letter, read in the spring of 1960 into the records of the New York State Commission of Investigation.

This futile appeal to the law, she wrote, had been followed by one last desperate fling on the husband's part. He had managed to scrape together $1,000 and left home, headed for the crap game. This time, he vowed, he was really going to hit the jackpot. His wife knew better. She followed him to the street; she grabbed his arm and tugged at him, crying, imploring him to come back home with the money his family so desperately needed. While this domestic dispute was taking place on the sidewalk, a Syracuse patrolman drove up to the curb in a patrol car. The wife turned and appealed to him.

"I told the policeman that my husband had $1,000 on his person and that he was headed for a gambling place," she wrote. "He had just lost $450 a few days before, gambling; I was determined to stop him from going any further.

"The policeman took my husband aside and talked to him a short time privately, and then the policeman came to me and asked if it would be all right if my husband took $100—would it be all right if I let him go then.

"As it turned out, I let him go, but instead of $100, he took $250. My husband told me later the policeman drove him to the gambling establishment in the police car right after I left. My husband said he gave the policeman $10 for driving him to the gambling place."

Capsuled in this anecdote is one of the great, overriding issues of our time—the domination of the law by forces of the lawless. For the shocking impact of this modern triangle of the professional gambler, the sucker victim, and the grafting cop lies the fact, not that it is unique, but that it is commonplace. It is a part of the face of America from coast to coast, and the wife in Syracuse who turned to the law for help and found it a shill for mobsters is a human symbol whose experience has a recognizable unversality. The illicit partnership of the law and the lawless, making a helpless victim of the public, has been exposed from Massachusetts to Florida, from Florida to California. It is a conspiracy that exists as surely in towns of 5,000 as it does in the teeming cities, and it expresses a plain fact—that bribery and corruption have become one of America's greatest industries.

Anyone who is inclined to boggle at the truth of this brutal statement needs only to turn to the records of recent years that document beyond all shadow of doubt what has happened to American society. The partnership of the overworld and the underworld, first formed on a national scale by the illicit millions Prohibition put into the hands of the mobs, has grown stronger and more meancing with time. It is a partnership that is now nourished by another fountain of wealth—the nation-wide gambling industry whose bankroll dwarfs what gangsters derived from bootlegging. This partnership operates on the brazen assumption that every man has his price, that it is possible to buy protection for everything from making book to committing murder. This wealth is used to influence the cop on the beat, the police chief at headquarters—and the politicians who control both.

The magnitude of the underworld gambling industry, a colossus larger than many legitimate industries, has been emphasized in every official study of the problem. One of the best of these was the little-noted report issued in 1957 by the Massachusetts Crime Commission. The commission devoted four years to its task; it questioned bookmakers, gamblers, mobsters of every stripe; it examined the problems of law enforcement and politics; and in the end it came to conclusions, usually understated and expressed with legalistic restraint, that are truly shocking in their implications. Its "basic finding," the commission wrote, was this: "*Organized crime has evolved into a state of society that amounts to lawlessness.*"

The commission, leaning over backwards to be conservative, tried to estimate the total underworld gambling revenue in Massachusetts and came up with a figure so huge it seems incredible—but a figure, the commission was convinced, so understated it did not convey the full truth. The figure was two billion dollars a year. On this gross play, profits in the various rackets ranged from 5 to 50 per cent, with a net take to the underworld of hundreds of millions of dollars a year. The commission, emphasizing the enormity of a $2 billion annual illegal gambling business, wrote: "For the year 1954, retail sales here by every establishment having a payroll of any kind totaled $5,202,282,000. The commission believes that the unlawful revenues of organized gambling reach at least two-fifths of this figure for legitimate, essential business."

In another comparison, the commission added graphic emphasis to the issue. It pointed out that the gross revenue of the retail food business, the largest single trade in the state, amounted to only $1,280,372,000. Reduced to the simplest and most understandable terms, what these figures meant was simply this: the public of Massachusetts was gambling nearly two dollars for every one dollar spent for food.

How could such a business run undisturbed, in open defiance of the law? Common sense dictates an inevitable answer, and the Massachusetts commission stated it in explicit terms.

"It seems to have been a universal finding by crime survey commissions that organized illegal gambling could not exist within a community without the knowledge and protection of the local police," it wrote. "For all practical purposes that is a fair statement. . . . The existence of an illegal gambling operation is as apparent as any other type of retail business. The place to which customers come, such as a horse room, the location of a card or dice game or of pinball machines, is more than apparent; it is obvious. The idea that games float to hide from police is more fiction that fact. Gaming operators have told the commission that they move to avoid complaint, not arrest. . . .

"Protection is a state that occurs as frequently by the demand of the police as by the offer of the racketeer. . . . The universal complaint among gaming operators is that the demands have been becoming increasingly exorbitant. Some have told the Commission that the price of protection has reached the stage where illegal gambling is *police business instead of bookie business.*"

Behind the venality of police, the commission found,

lies the true source of corruption—the unholy alliance of the underworld and politics. A net annual gambling take running into hundreds of millions of dollars buys a lot of votes and influence, and even if a policeman wants to be honest, as many policemen do, he frequently does not dare because the elected officials who outrank him are obviously obligated.

"Politics creates and encourages more conditions adverse to law enforcement than any other single cause," the Massachusetts commission wrote. "Politics interferes with law enforcement at the state, county, and local levels. . . . The most important connection between the racketeer and the politician is in the matter of campaign expenses. . . . The task of running for public office is an expensive one. This is particularly true since the advent of television."

The Massachusetts commission cited one vivid and fairly typical example of the link that weds crime and politics. "In addition to the matter of campaign expenses," it wrote, "there is also the important element of the need for workers in a campaign. Bookmakers and leaders in the rackets have a great many hangers-on who can be made available along with automobiles for such activities. One investigator with the Commission witnessed a well-known gambling operator, who served time in State Prison on a murder charge, paying workers $20 apiece in a barroom for services rendered in behalf of one seeking the nomination for District Attorney."

Such is the magnitude of the gambling evil, such the links of crime to the law and to politics that were exposed in Massachusetts alone. The findings are highly typical of conditions that exist across the nation. Time and again, in state after state, one finds the same system, the same pattern, the same lame alibis for official inaction. To anyone who studies the situation and tries to face its implications unflinchingly, it becomes obvious that here is a national malaise gnawing at the very vitals of democratic government. For when the lawless can bribe and dominate the law, the worst elements of society, not the best, have most influence. And when one projects the $2-billion-a-year gambling racket in Massachusetts on a national scale, the investment in corruption becomes so huge it seems almost to rival the federal budget.

For the magnitude of this tally of dishonesty one can cite impressive sources. In 1960 Attorney General William G. Rogers estimated the total income of the rackets in America at about $20 billion a year, of which half was represented by gambling. J. Edgar Hoover, director of the Federal Bureau of Investigation, put the racket toll at about $22 billion and also estimated that about half, or $11 billion came from gambling.

The analysis that is probably the most detailed and authoritative is only a little more conservative. This figure comes from Milton R. Wessel, the energetic New York corporation lawyer who headed the short-lived Attorney General's Special Group on Organized Crime. Wessel devoted a lot of attention to developing an estimate of just how big the rackets were, and his approach, it must be emphasized, was very conservative.

Let's look, for example, at the manner in which he arrived at his estimate of the size of illegal horse-race bookmaking. In countries that have legalized off-track betting, the ratio of money bet away from the track to that bet at the tracks is never less than two to one and frequently goes as high as five to one—and in addition usually there is still some illegal wagering. The Massachusetts Crime Commission pointed out that the lowest estimate it obtained from the gambling fraternity itself is that four dollars will be bet away from the tracks for every dollar bet at them. Bookies in Massachusetts considered a five to one ratio conservative, but the commission, determined to err on the side of caution, used only a three to one ratio in compiling its estimate of a $2-billion-a-year state gambling racket. Wessel, similarly cautious, adopted the same three to one ratio in figuring the national horse-racing play of the bookies. In 1959 legal pari-mutuel betting in the nation amounted to approximately $3 billion; on this basis, Wessel computed that $9 billion was being wagered with the bookies away from the tracks.

Even this sum, huge as it is, represents only the lesser part of bookie business. The public generally suffers from the misapprehension that bookies derive the greater part of their trade from horse racing. The fact is that they do not. Investigations have shown this, and the bookies themselves list betting on sports as their number one item of business. Baseball and football, including wagering on pools in which profits to the operators can run as high as 92 per cent, were both estimated by Wessel to be more remunerative to the bookie than horse racing, and basketball is not far behind. As Wessel pointed out, bets on sporting events usually involve larger sums of money than are wagered on the races. The horses lure the two dollar to five dollar bettor, but the least that is usually bet on a baseball game is ten dollars. In New York, investigators found that bookies shy from accepting large single bets on horse races, suspecting a possible fix, but they will accept virtually unlimited amounts on a baseball game. The New York probers uncovered one instance in which a bettor risked $10,000 on the outcome of a single ball game.

Wessel and his experts concluded that baseball nets

the bookies half again as much as horse racing and that football play is one-third larger. Wessel added to these figures an estimated $4 billion in fight and hockey bets. But he did not include any estimate of the money bet in slot machines and gambling casinos, legal in Nevada although illegal in most of the rest of the nation. This phase of gambling has been estimated as a $4 billion annual business; but even without this, Wessel and his aides came up with a shocking total. They concluded that the American public was spending *$46.5 billion a year* on all forms of illegal gambling—a figure larger than the defense budget!

This is the total turnover, the total "handle"—in other words, money that is bet and re-bet. Out of this huge flow of cash, Wessel and the experts on his crime task force, by using accepted minimal profit percentages for the various rackets, estimated that the underworld keeps about *$9 billion*. But, Wessel pointed out, this is not all clear profit. "Fully half of the syndicates' income from gambling" he stated flatly, "is earmarked for protection money paid to police and politicians."

Just what does a gross underworld gambling profit of $9 billion a year actually mean? In dealing with figures so grandiose that they evade the grasp of the imagination, one needs some solid basis of comparison. In recent years, the total production of the auto industry has borne a wholesale price tag of between eight and nine billion dollars. In other words, the underworld's gross annual gambling *profit* is roughly comparable in an average year to *the entire income* of American automobile manufacturing, one of the basic bellwethers of national prosperity.

Figures so huge nonetheless almost defy comprehension. Perhaps one of the best ways to demonstrate this influence is to reduce it from the general to the specific and by a few graphic examples show the extent and depth of corruption.

In Richmond, Virginia, federal authorities in March, 1960, uncovered the activities of a numbers operator who was handling $2 million a year in bets. Records showed that, during one four-year period, he had averaged $2.2 million a year. Testimony before a federal grand jury indicated that Richmond policemen were being paid from $3,500 to $5,000 a month to let the system operate. The federal jury subpoenaed 105 Richmond cops, more than a quarter of the total force of 392, and 60 of them reportedly claimed the privilege of the Fifth Amendment against possible self-incrimination and refused to testify.

In Miami, Florida, in this same winter of 1960, Mayor Robert King High launched an investigation of a $100,000-a-week Bolita operation, a form of numbers play. He charged that 10 per cent of the proceeds were going to local police payoffs. Though Bolita is a nickels-and-dimes operation, the gambling game of the extremely poor, the weekly play indicated that this racket alone involved a cash flow of more than $5 million a year.

In New Orleans, Louisiana, despite specific and thorough disclosures by the Kefauver Committee ten years earlier, the Carlos Marcello mob, unhampered by a law that sees no evil, hears no evil, and speaks no evil, was still running wide-open rackets of every kind—slot machines, handbooks, and huge gambling casinos. Some of them were flourishing exactly where they were when Kefauver exposed them. The Marcello combine had grown so wealthy and so powerful that it could funnel literally millions of dollars into the purchase of hotels, motels, and other legitimate businesses.

An extra dimension is given to this portrait of corruption when one examines some of the most important evidence compiled in recent years, developed during the spring and summer of 1960 by the New York State Commission of Investigation. In a series of hearings the New York commission probed deeply into the interrelation of gambling, crime, and corruption. Its findings are especially revealing because they are based on so much specific evidence, uncovered in sweeping raids conducted by agents of the commission and the New York State Police in late October, 1959. Months of preparation preceded the raids; they were so well organized that one hundred major books across the entire breadth of the state were knocked off at precisely the same minute in one afternoon; and the detailed records seized in the surprise swoop eliminated guesswork from estimates and provided a solid, factual picture of the big-money game of the underworld: bookmaking.

The New York commission turned a strong and significant spotlight on a little-regarded aspect of the gambling racket—the manner in which it extends even into the grassroots. We have become callous to the spectacle of crime and corruption in our cities; we have assumed that the rural scene is purer. This, the New York commission showed, is a false assumption. Take, for example, the town of Falconer. It lies in the Buffalo area near the Pennsylvania border. It has a population of less than 5,000. Yet it supported a flourishing bookmaking operation with interstate ties to Minneapolis, Detroit, Washington, and Wilkes-Barre, Pennsylvania. Falconer was not an exception; it was typical. The New York commission found that it was almost impossible to find a municipality of 10,000 persons without a bookmaking operation.

There were many other specific disclosures that emanated from the New York hearings. Here are some of the high points:

1. The hundred raided books—that is, the hundred

central bookmaking operations—handled bets totaling $250 million annually. Criminal experts, after examining the records of many raided books throughout the years, usually consider that these profit margins are conservative: 15 per cent on horse-racing, baseball, basketball and the fights, and 25 per cent on football. The New York commission in all its official estimates used an ultra-conservative 10 per cent margin-of-profit figure, and on this basis computed that the underworld was clearing $25 million a year from these hundred raided books alone. But this was by no means the full take. The raided books were not the only ones operating in upstate New York; they were simply all that the commission and State Police could raid in a single afternoon. After months of labor sifting out the clues contained in 25,000 pages of reports, the commission in late November, 1960, disseminated to municipalities in the state all the information it had gathered about bookmakers and their locations. The statistics were awesome. The commission identified 2,150 bookie locations in 206 communities located in 54 of New York's 62 counties, and New York City *was not even included.* There were 347 spots in Buffalo alone, 196 in Rochester, 100 in Syracuse. Such figures make it obvious that the $250 million annual business of the one hundred raided books must be multiplied many times before one can begin to strike any true total for the traffic in New York.

2. There is literally a small army of racketeers wedded to the interests of crime. Statistics of the New York commission showed that, on an average, which included establishments both large and small, raided books employed at least ten runners, or a total force of 1,000. If such a ratio should hold true for the 2,150 bookie sites pinpointed by the commission, this would mean an army of 21,500 rack-

eteers operating in upstate New York. Such a figure, huge as it is, is not fantastic. In 1955, the Massachusetts Crime Commission reported that the most reliable estimate it could get showed an army of 10,000 bookies working in Massachusetts alone at the time. From the bookie industry itself one gets estimates like the one published by Roger Kahn, sports editor of *Newsweek,* in the summer of 1960 —that throughout the nation as a whole gambling supports 50,000 master books and some 400,000 small fry.

3. Commission investigators established that, in just eight weeks, one Canadian bookie with whom the upstate New York boys were doing a layoff business made a *profit of $500,000 on baseball play alone.*

"This is *not* an estimate," William D. Walsh, assistant counsel to the commission, declared during the 1960 hearings. "We accurately determined this during the course of the investigation." Analysis by expert accountants showed that the twelve largest books among the one hundred raided did a gross annual business ranging from $5 million to $10 million apiece. Ever hear of the town of Watervliet? It is a small city of 15,000 tucked away in the Troy-Rensselaer industrial area not far from Albany. When New York raiders struck the book operated there by James and Frank Cocca, they were fortunate enough to seize records containing details of the gross play for the last thirty-two days. In that time, just a little over a month, $512,271 had been bet with the Coccas—an average of $16,000 a day, or $4,992,000 a year.

4. The tremendous illicit business was being conducted almost as openly as a supermarket. Walsh, who masterminded the New York investigation, testified that some books had operated at the same location for thirty years. Some of them and their exact addresses had been identified

in testimony before the Kefauver Committee nearly ten years earlier but this public exposure had not impaired their racket or induced them to move even across the street. Across the state, commission investigators found representatives of the law unable to give any satisfactory explanation of why they allowed multi-million-dollar rackets to run wide-open right under their noses. In Syracuse, the *Herald-Journal* conducted a months-long crusade against the gambling rackets. It printed more than 200 front-page stories. In one series it named the exact blocks in which each of more than twenty gambling spots was located. Police, as usual, promised a vigorous crackdown, but more than a year later, when the state commission and the state police went into Syracuse, they found ten of the spots still flourishing exactly where the *Herald-Journal* had said they were. Even worse, if possible, was the situation in Buffalo. So wide open was this city, the second largest in New York State, that one of the commission's investigators on his first night in town was steered to a spot where he could get gambling "action" by a policeman in uniform. Subsequently, the commission discovered that a desk lieutenant in Police Headquarters was actually running his own book.

When one finds a police lieutenant doubling as a bookie, one sees clearly the link between the law and the lawless. Some will argue, of course, that gambling is just a peccadillo; that gambling graft is really "honest" graft; that the law is not corrupted to the core by it because it does not involve the protection of any heinous crime. This argument is based upon myths that have been widely promulgated by the takers to justify their taking—and that have been widely swallowed by the press and the public. These myths would have us believe that the professional gambler is a "gentleman" crook furnishing a genteel service to gentlemen who wish to experience the thrill of hazarding their money; and so there is really nothing wrong if a cop takes a little "honest" graft for permitting these "gentlemen" to run a racket that is not really a racket, but almost a kindly service to mankind.

No defense of dishonesty could be more dishonest. It should be obvious that the instant a policeman or a public official takes, he takes—period. He is obligated. He is tied by his own thievery to the thieves with whom he deals and he has no choice, since he dare not risk self-exposure, but to support and sanction them in all their doings. Of course mobsters, even major ones, do at times get arrested. But anyone who has studied their records knows that they are hardly ever convicted. A man must apparently climb to the heights of a Frank Costello or a Joe Adonis, and then run into literally national exposure like that provided by the Kefauver Committee, before the law becomes incensed enough to send him to jail.

The virtual immunity that gamblers enjoy from prosecution is of crucial importance once one realizes the complete fallacy of that myth that the professional gambler is a gentleman crook. The well-documented record says that he is not. He is a professional criminal, all too often ready for any deed from pimping to peddling narcotics to committing murder.

Scratch a bookie and you'll find all kinds of encrustations of filth. The Massachusetts Crime Commission turned the spotlight on the pasts of seventeen of these "nice fellows" selected at random. It found that their offenses ranged from attempted rape to suspicion of murder. One "nice fellow" had a police record thirty-three offenses long, including assault and battery, counterfeiting, breaking and entering, possession of burglars' tools, and assault with intent to rob while carrying a dangerous weapon. Another had been arrested forty times for offenses including jail break, violation of the White Slave Traffic Act, and armed robbery.

Even more striking was the dilemma in which the Massachusetts commission found itself with respect to what has been called "the crime of the century"—the Brink's holdup, in which an armed gang wearing Halloween masks escaped with $2.5 million in cash and securities. So intertwined were the strands of gambling and crime that the Massachusetts commission was plagued by the fear that, in seeking evidence about gambling, it might inadvertently offer immunity from prosecution to a Brink's robber. The commission on one occasion did almost fall into the trap. As it later reported, it "did summon Vincent Costa, one of those convicted for his part in the robbery, to question him concerning his part and the part of his brother-in-law, Anthony Pino, another Brink's defendant, in the Treasury Balance lottery operations." (This is a lottery in which the winning number is determined by the last five digits of the published figures of the United States Treasury balance for the day.) Fortunately for the commission, Costa took the Fifth Amendment against self-incrimination; but the ties of gamblers to the sensational holdup illustrate that the professional gambler is a cheap thug who will not balk at any type of crime, low or high, that leads to a buck.

What was true in Massachusetts was equally true in New York. Everywhere the New York raiders went, with few exceptions, they found bookies armed to the teeth. "Whenever we made a wiretap," says Bill Walsh, the stocky, hard-driving field general of the New York probe, "we came upon the trail of all kinds of crime—petty thieves, prostitutes, pimping, abortions. Either the gambler himself was mixed up in such business or his immediate hangers-on were, and they were discussing their affairs right over his phone."

In Syracuse detectives listened to a series of conversations between a typical mobster and an eighteen-year-old girl with whom he had been sleeping. He was trying to persuade the girl that they could both make money from the use of her talents.

"I had four guys here today who offered me a yard and a half ($1,500) for a night with you," he told her.

"You mean you'd want me to do *that*?" the girl protested.

"No, of course not," said her lover slyly. "You don't know enough about sex."

To a girl who obviously had been priding herself on her knowledge in this field, this belittlement was a real affront.

"What do you mean I don't know enough about sex?" she bridled.

"You still don't know how to handle four guys like these," said her boyfriend.

"W-e-ll," said the girl hesitantly, "what were they like? Were they good-looking?"

"See!" shouted lover boy. "That's just what I mean. You don't know enough about sex. What difference does it make what they look like? You've got to get it through your head that this is a *business*."

Eventually the young girl agreed to turn prostitute for her pimp-lover.

"This was a real, cheap, low-down crumb," Bill Walsh says, struggling to find words adequate to express his contempt. "He fancied himself such a bigshot. He'd brag about a few bucks he'd picked up in a crap game the night before, or some cheap swindle he was working, and all the time he was talking this girl into turning to prostitution for him. This was just one example of what we found all over the state. The scum of the earth gather around a bookie and a bookie's phone."

This has been demonstrated again and again in one of the most nefarious rackets of our times—narcotics. You will frequently hear it protested that there is really nothing wrong with taking a little "honest" graft from a bookmaker; but that it is different, of course, if a cop takes "dirty" graft from a narcotics peddler. Such protestations are hypocrisy's wasted breath, for the plain fact is that there is no difference: the bookie and the narcotics peddler are frequently one and the same person.

One of the most recent and vivid examples is to be found in the career of Harry Stromberg, alias Nig Rosen. Stromberg had been an associate of Louis (Lepke) Buchalter, the master extortionist of the New York mob during the Thirties. Lepke went to the electric chair in Sing Sing as a result of the Murder Inc. probe, but Stromberg lived to enjoy bigger and better things. He became a major gambler in the New York-Philadelphia area; he reaped a harvest from gambling casinos in New Jersey, Florida, Las Vegas, and Cuba. In the early 1950's, Sol Gelb, alias Solly Gordon, who earlier had financed his international narcotics traffic with the aid of such gamblers as Benny (Buggsy) Siegel and Dutch Goldberg, found that he needed heavy cash for expansion and turned for help to Stromberg. Stromberg actually took over the financial end of the business and made heavy deposits in numbered accounts in Swiss banks. From 1951 to 1955, Stromberg and eighteen associates who were subsequently convicted with him imported hundreds of kilograms of heroin, using a chain that ran from Turkey through laboratories in France and smugglers in Mexico, Cuba, and Canada. In one eighteen-month period, the Stromberg gambling-narcotics combine imported fifty pounds of heroin a month through the ports of New York and Boston alone. Some of its individual shipments had a value in this country of five million dollars.

An equally colossal operation was masterminded by Vito Genovese, the Mafia chieftain who has been called "the kingmaker of the underworld." As the Federal Bureau of Narcotics showed at Genovese's trial, his favorite technique featured a direct pairing of policy and narcotics. Time and again Genovese's mob muscled into new areas in New York City's East Harlem and the Bronx. Its first procedure was to establish a neighborhood policy bank; its next, to use numbers runners to peddle narcotics. The size of this operation may be gleaned from the fact that Genovese's mob used its combined gambling-narcotics millions to import heroin from Mexico and Cuba and distribute it throughout the United States. Through its policy outlets in New York, the mob handled its own retailing; outside the city, it sold drugs in huge, wholesale lots to distributors in Cleveland, Chicago, Philadelphia, Las Vegas, and Los Angeles.

Such is the record that demonstrates that every crime in the book, not excluding murder, can be laid directly at the door of "the nice fellows" who oblige and whet the appetite of millions of Americans for gambling. It is not stretching the truth to say that the bookie is the agent who invests the funds of the two dollar bettor and the fifty cent numbers player in the pay-off and corruption of public officials on the one hand and the financing of rackets like narcotics peddling on the other.

A Brooklyn grand jury that made an extensive, special study of gambling in 1958 came to the conclusion that gambling in all its forms represents the treasure chest of the underworld and finances every other kind of racket. In a strong and clearly worded presentment, the jury said:

"Gambling is the very heartbeat of organized crime both on a local and national scale. . . . From the evidence presented to us, we state categorically that gambling crimes are linked on innumerable occasions with the most obnoxious criminal enterprises known to man. The public may think of the bookmaker in the corner candy store as an innocent betting commissioner operating a legitimate business. We have heard the evidence. We know otherwise. Actually, if you scratch the professional operator of gambling ventures, you find the narcotics peddler, the loan shark, the dice-game operator, the white slaver, the murderer. Brooklyn has been the scene of a number of unsolved gangland homicides over the past few years. Almost every one of those killings is involved with gambling ventures in one form or another. In one case where seven narcotics dealers were convicted in Kings County last year, six were actively engaged in gambling activities, including bookmaking and policy, which they used as the source of funds for their deadly trade in narcotics."

Murder on an organized and wholesale scale, as the Brooklyn grand jury indicated, has become a sinister by-product of the multi-billion dollar gambling rackets. The struggle for control of such a tempting pot of gold keeps the underworld in lethal turmoil. Ever since the Kefauver probe of 1950-51 exposed the old order and led to the dethronement of Frank Costello and Joe Adonis, the emperors of the East, a new war of the underworld has been waged for dominion over the gambling rackets and their enormous revenues. The evidences of this war are indisputable; they have been displayed for all to see in the bodies dumped indiscriminately on the streets.

Only the more gory and the more sensational executions make newspaper headlines. The public remembers such dramatic items as the mid-morning slaying in a midtown New York barbershop of Albert Anastasia, the Lord High Executioner of the old Murder Inc. Or the midnight execution of Anthony (Little Augie Pisano) Carfano, onetime ruler of the Brooklyn rackets, in his Cadillac near LaGuardia Airport. But the warfare on the lower echelons of the mob produces a plethora of little-known victims whose violent passages rate only a few inconspicuous lines of type and are quickly forgotten.

New York City police statistics do not segregate unsolved gangland murders from other murders. Police contend that, unless a murder is solved, no one can be positive what motivated it, but homicide detectives and other investigators privately agree that the toll of the last ten years is positively staggering. In that period there have been at least 200 unsolved gangland slayings in New York City alone, and most investigators place the number closer to 300. Some of these executions, it is true, stem from rivalry for control of narcotics or other rackets; but the vast majority, as the Brooklyn grand jury discovered, have ties that stretch back into gambling, around which all else seems to pivot.

Such, then, are the inevitable final wages of the "gentlemen's" racket. It is nonsense for police officials and law-enforcement authorities to repeat the weary old refrain that they didn't know. Public officials can't help knowing. Yet across the nation many of the very mobsters who were identified ten years ago in Kefauver Committee testimony are still doing business at the same stand. All that has happened is that they have grown more wealthy and more powerful than they were in 1951. When even the shock wave of public reaction that the Kefauver Committee produced cannot stir the law to its duty, when even page-one exposés in the newspapers of city after city cannot enlighten it, one begins to get some idea of the tight clutch of corruption. It is a hold so strong that not even public exposure and embarrassment can shake it. And for as long as it endures, just one thing is certain—a two-dollar bet means murder.

2

RACKET IN A GOLDFISH BOWL

BOOKMAKING, the most remunerative of the gambling rackets, has the advantage of a certain degree of secrecy; yet, actually, despite the protestations of police that it is so hard to ferret out, it runs virtually in a goldfish bowl.

The paradox is implicit in the very nature of the business. A bookie handles most of his transactions by telephone, with a minimum of personal contact, and the telephone is essentially a private and secretive device. If a bookie's needs could be limited simply to answering a phone and taking bets, he would probably have the world's most cop-proof racket; but unfortunately for him, to operate his business, he needs certain vital services, and these services are clear giveaways to his activity.

The pressing needs of a bookie are three: He must get "the line"; he must be able to "lay off" dangerously heavy play; he must get fast results from the racetrack or sporting event.

Getting "the line" means that the bookie must have constant access to an expert and recognized handicapper who can keep him up to the minute on just what the points or odds are on a horse race, a baseball game, a basketball game, or the weekend's college and professional football competition.

In America today there is just one "line" that is recognized nationally as *the* line. In popular parlance, it is known as "the Minneapolis line," and if you take a look at the sports pages of your favorite newspaper, you are almost certain to find recorded there "the Minneapolis line" giving the point spread on the athletic contests of the moment. A typical example is a "Football Line" taken from a New York daily newspaper. This lists the favored team, the number of points it was favored by, and the underdog. For example, in the line one Saturday in the fall of 1960, Pennsylvania was favored by three points over Dartmouth, Duke by six over Maryland, Yale by sixteen over Brown, and Notre Dame by three over Purdue, to cite just a few. This means that the favored team is an even-money bet, given the handicap of this number of points. The prominent display of such "lines" on the sports pages of the daily press is an inestimable journalistic service, disclosing the findings of the nation's betting "bible" to alumni engaging in friendly bets—and also to the bookies and their patrons.

The "Minneapolis Line" is the product of a firm known as Athletic Publications Inc., run by Leo Hirshfield, a short, gray-haired man in his sixties. Hirshfield maintains a four-room suite in a large Minneapolis office building. In one room are several desks and a battery of telephones. At each desk and phone sits a man, before him a list containing the printed code numbers representing Hirshfield clients who may be calling for the latest odds. A staff of eighteen persons mans the telephones, runs the office, and sets the point spread and odds on sporting events all over the nation.

Each Monday, Hirshfield mails out to his clients a schedule of the week's coming events. In the football season he distributes 25,000 to 30,000 lists each week. Since most customers need more than one copy, this probably means that he has 8,000 to 10,000 clients during this peak period of the year. Throughout the remainder of the week, the customers call by telephone to get what Hirshfield calls his "early line," his "mid-week line," and his "late line."

The client calling for information always identifies himself by his code number—never by name. For instance, "102" may call from Cincinnati. The Hirshfield employee answering the phone makes a check by the symbol "102" showing service rendered; then he reads off the odds as fast as tongue can clack the numbers.

The man at the other end of the phone would be hopelessly lost if he did not have the printed Hirshfield list on which to jot down the odds in the exact order that they are given. The printed schedules, so essential to the service, cost Hirshfield subscribers 20 cents each; the phone updating of "the line" costs from $15 to $30 a week, depending on the amount of advice a client seeks.

Hirshfield founded Athletic Publications in 1940, when he bought the former Gorham Press and expanded the business. For twenty years, with a minimum of difficulty, he has supplied the gambling industry of the country with a vital service. In 1957 he encountered some minor trouble with authorities in Minneapolis and moved his enterprise to Davenport, Iowa; but within two years, affairs in Minnesota righted themselves and he moved back to his native city. Indignation comes easily to Hirshfield when anyone suggests that his business is tied closely to the illicit gambling industry of the country.

"This is a legitimate business," he insists, with some

heat. "I don't know who uses it. I simply provide a service. I can't regulate what people do with the information I give them."

Myles Lord, Attorney General of Minnesota, told the New York State Commission of Investigation that Hirshfield's premise of legitimacy is indeed a hard legal nut to crack. The handicapper, he pointed out, is not making bets or taking bets; he is, as he says, simply providing a service; and in giving out information to out-of-state callers who seek it, he is not fracturing any local or state law.

So Hirshfield continues to run wide open, issuing "the Minneapolis line" to "clients" all over the nation. Some of them, he insists, are sports writers who want his views. Some are heavy bettors who figure his service is a valuable guide to them in contemplated gambles. Many—though Hirshfield insists he has no personal knowledge of this—are professional bookies.

The master handicapper's posture of complete innocence received some rough handling in the New York probe. When Eliot H. Lumbard, chief counsel of the New York commission, and Bill Walsh, his top assistant, began to map their drive against upstate New York bookies, it occurred to them that the quickest and best way to get on the spoor of their quarry would be to check the Minneapolis clearing house of "the line," where most of the contacts inevitably would have to show. Walsh, who formerly served as an Assistant U.S. Attorney and helped to prepare the federal narcotics case against Vito Genovese, decided to take a detective with him and pay a surprise visit on Hirshfield.

The two New Yorkers walked in unheralded in midafternoon of a weekday during the basketball season. Basketball play is considerably lighter than football, and one reason is that the game is greatly suspect. A brooding bribery scandal has been hovering over the professional game for several years. Rumors have been widely prevalent that professional players have been "taking" to throw games or rig the point margin, and there have been reports that certain referees are corrupt—as gamblers say, "We own their whistle." The general public has not been sufficiently aware of the smothered scandal to stop betting on professional basketball completely; but the bookies, as the New York commission found when it later probed into gambling in Buffalo, are more sensitive. Many of them have wiped pro basketball off their books—in other words they have refused to accept bets—because they are convinced that many of the games are being rigged. All of this has reduced Hirshfield's mid-winter business. He mails out only about 15,000 basketball line schedules each week compared to 25,000 to 30,000 in football season. Walsh and his detective were calling at one of the slowest times of the year and at one of the slowest times of the day and week; but even so the Hirshfield office was buzzing.

The phones kept shrilling with a rapid-fire sequence of calls; Walsh counted twenty-three in fifteen minutes. Hirshfield employees answered the calls, checked off the code numbers on their lists, ran swiftly through the latest "line."

Walsh noted and was intrigued by one procedure. When Hirshfield's handicappers sniff the reek of a fix, as they did in the college basketball scandals in the early 1950's, for example, they warn their customers by putting the point spread they quote "in a box."

"Thus, while we were there," Walsh told the New York commission, "we heard one game which was called 'five, in a box.' " Anyone studying "the line" in 1949-1950 would have known of the college basketball fix at once—and well in advance of official action—because he "would have noticed repeatedly . . . all New York games were 'in a box.' "

The New York investigator was anxious to find out how Hirshfield arrives at his "line," how he determines whether figures should be put "in a box." The stocky, square-faced master of "the Minneapolis line" has been quoted as saying that he doesn't know the first thing about handicapping, that he relies on his expert and dedicated staff. Obviously, Walsh found, Hirshfield's information is gathered from a wide variety of sources. He subscribes to daily newspapers in every section of the nation and to an even greater number of college publications. Each fall, for instance, he writes to college publicity bureaus for their forecasts and information on their teams, and his Athletic Publications Inc. regularly receives the daily releases from a vast majority of the nation's top schools. From such sources, details can be culled about injuries, condition, and attitude, all key factors in determining the performance of a squad on the gridiron on any given Saturday afternoon.

Hirshfield angrily denies that he has any contact with coaches or clubhouse personnel, but he does boast of a wide and friendly acquaintance among the leading sports writers of the nation. He points out that some top journalists do not hesitate to write at times for some of his various sports publications—a tie that, it would seem, might prove valuable on occasion in providing Hirshfield with inside information. In addition to all these sources Hirshfield has one other—and perhaps not the least of the lot. Some bookies testified in the New York probe that Hirshfield not only supplies them with "the line"; he picks their brains for information. Since a bookie is a prime repository for scuttlebutt—and since he is apt sooner than anyone to smell a local fix that can cost him money—his knowledge might well be at times invaluable to Hirshfield.

In any event, pooling the data obtained from all these sources, Hirshfield's experts make their prognostications, battle out their conflicting opinions, and finally come up with "the line" that is to be issued.

The identity of these "clients" was the principal concern of Bill Walsh. As he later testified before the New York commission, he felt that a list of Hirshfield's customers would provide "the key to the whole conspiracy"; but when he asked for such a list, Hirshfield absolutely refused to give it out. "And so far," Walsh concluded, "no one has made him."

Hirshfield is not, of course, the only purveyor of a "line," and he is not the only one who feels that the names of the gentlemen with whom he does business are none of the law's affair. Walsh encountered the same secretive attitude when he went on to Chicago, where the Angel-Kaplan Service runs what is generally regarded as the number two "line" in the country. Here, too, Walsh found it impossible to get a line on the customer. But he did at least discover one bit of evidence that illustrated graphically just what a huge business running even a second-rate "line" can be.

On a wall of the Angel-Kaplan office hung a large map of the United States, stabbed with pins like a pin cushion. "Each pin indicates a customer for a different type of line all over the United States," Walsh testified. "There are thousands of pins in this map."

Though the New York commission did not try to estimate the profit of the Hirshfield and Angel-Kaplan operations, it is obvious that each must be a multi-million-dollar business. Even if one completely disregards Hirshfield's revenue from his mailed line sheets and his athletic publications, even if one assumes that he averages only 5,000 steady customers a year at $20 a week (both ultra-conservative figures since his full service costs $30 and he has at least double the number of customers during the peak season), one arrives at an estimated gross of at least $5.2 million a year. All this out of one office employing only eighteen persons. Such are the rewards of the free enterprise that supplies the first of a bookie's most pressing needs.

The second of the three musts involves money in even more fantastic proportions. This is the loot of the "layoff." Inextricably mixed up with the "layoff" is an item known in the trade as "vigorish." This is the bookie's guaranteed edge. On horse racing, for example, the "payout" is determined by the odds quoted on the pari-mutuel machines at the tracks. But, as the Massachusetts commission pointed out, the tracks always take a percentage "off the top" to pay taxes to the state and defray the costs of running the racing plants. In Massachusetts, this "takeout" averages 15½ per cent before the pari-mutuel odds are figured. In illegal betting, the bookie pays out at the same rate as the pari-mutuel machines, except in cases where the track odds strike him as onerous. On an exceptional long shot, for example, the track odds might be thirty to one but no self-respecting bookie would dream of giving his customers such a break. The bookies set the top figure they will pay, certainly no more than twenty to one regardless of the track odds, and they pocket the difference. They also pocket that 15½ per cent "off the top" though they have no race track to maintain, no pari-mutuel tax to pay, nothing to worry about—except, of course, "protection."

Such is "vigorish," a lusty percentage that is always working in the bookie's favor. No matter what the form of betting, the bookie's "vigorish" is always there. Take a look, for example, at what happens on a heavyweight championship prize fight. The fight game has been so discredited by fixes that, as the New York probe showed, less than 1 per cent of a bookie's business is now represented by prizefight bets; but a heavyweight championship bout, the supreme attraction of the sport, still lures heavy "action." Typical of what happens in such cases was the return bout between Ingemar Johansson and Floyd Patterson in the summer of 1960. The early odds were "6-5, pick 'em." This meant that, if you liked Patterson, you had to wager six dollars on the chance of winning five dollars; similarly, if you liked Johansson, you had to put up six dollars to win five dollars. A bookie having the same amount of money bet on each fighter was rolling in clover. Obviously, only one man could win, and it was a matter of complete indifference to the bookie who that winner might be, since his books would be neatly balanced, and he would have to pay out only eleven dollars for every twelve dollars he took in.

Clearly, with "vigorish" going so vigorously for him, the only time disaster can overtake a bookie, aside from the unlikely hazards of the law, comes if he allows himself to be overloaded on one betting proposition—one horse, one fighter, one football team. This elemental fact of bookmaking life has led to the development of the "layoff." If one bookie is overloaded on a horse, he hunts another bookie not faced with the same problem with whom he can bet some of the play on the dangerous nag. This is known as "spreading the play," and bookies have a mutual understanding to help each other out in this manner, each balancing his books and letting "vigorish" guarantee his profits.

Simple "layoff" problems can be handled on a neighborhood or regional basis; but on major events, with heavy play, this is obviously impossible. Huge money, sometimes millions of dollars, may ride on a single event. This means that the "layoff" operation must be bankrolled heavily; it means, almost inevitably, that there has to be a national clearing house, to which small and medium bookies all over the nation can resort in their need. Throughout the decade of the 1940's and into the early 1950's the czar of the nation's "layoff" industry was Frank Erickson, the roly-poly master New York bookie who had his headquarters and accounting house just across the Hudson River in Bergen County, New Jersey. There Erickson handled "layoff" play from all of the forty-eight states. When the McCarran Committee, predecessor of the Kefauver Committee, caught up with Erickson in early 1950, the law finally stepped in. Erickson went to jail, and the scene of activity shifted. But the system remained the same.

That system and the manner in which it still runs was described in testimony in the New York probe by Joseph P. Manners, of Miami, Florida, a former Assistant U.S. Attorney and special assistant to the head of the Criminal Division of the Justice Department for thirteen Southern states. Manners headed the active field force under Milton Wessel—the unit that labored all too briefly from September, 1958, to May, 1959, on the national bookmaking problem.

Manners pointed out that the "layoff" begins with the $2 bettor who places his wager with the small-fry handbook operating from the corner newsstand. This $2 bettor likes Black Jack in the third at Hialeah. As the morning passes, it becomes obvious that other bettors in the neighborhood like Black Jack too, and the first thing the handbook knows his play is out of whack—he has $20 bet on Black Jack. So he contacts a larger book, one step up the ladder, and wagers $10 of the dangerous Black Jack play with him. Should this larger book find himself overloaded on Black Jack, he in turn tries to "lay off" the dangerous overload with the largest regional book, and if the play tilts the ledgers of the regional book a large part of the load will be transferred to one of the two national clearing houses that now provide this type of gambling insurance. The smaller of these is located in Biloxi, Mississippi; the larger, in the neighborhood of Covington, Kentucky.

Biloxi is a wide-open town. According to Manners, gambling is "the only source of economy it has. . . . You walk down the street and every store has a one-armed bandit [slot machine], contrary to state law. . . ." The "layoff" headquarters is located in what is known as "the 406 Club" at 406 Magnolia Street. The telephone number is Idlewood 2-2633, and this number was extremely popular with upstate New York bookies who kept calling it to "lay off" with someone called "P. J." Manners described the 406 Club as "a typical gambling joint. You walk right in. There are tables. The old-fashioned board. They give you the results, and it's open to the public. The public doesn't want to change it."

In trying to check up on the Biloxi operation, Manners testified, he wrote to the local police and asked for a report on the premises and the phone activity at the 406 Club. After a considerable lapse of time, this was the reply he got:

"Please pardon my delay in answering your letter. I have been out of office. The above is listed in the name of the 406 Club and this club is owned and operated by local boys whose reputation is, as far as I know, very good. If I can be of further service to you, please let me hear from you."

This bland official endorsement of "local boys" who were running an interstate gambling racket that stretched all the way from Biloxi to upstate New York and beyond, is typical of the lethargic forces of modern law. Yet, said Manners, "That phone averages over—I would say 1,500 calls a month going in."

Important as Biloxi is in the "layoff" operation, it handles only a tithe of the business that flows into the nation's major "layoff" center—the Newport-Covington area of Kentucky. Even in the days of Frank Erickson, Covington had begun to handle a heavy proportion of the play, as the Kefauver Committee found in 1951. Nothing has changed since that memorable exposé except that the rackets in Newport and Covington flourish even more rankly and prolifically today. Indeed, the New York commission pinpointed the Newport-Covington area, just a short taxi ride across the Ohio River from Cincinnati, as the "layoff" capital of the country. And it found that some of the same outfits exposed by Kefauver—the Ace Research Service and the New-Cov Bookkeeping Service, to cite just a couple—are still handling big "layoff" money, their locations, names, and businesses unchanged and unpurified.

To understand just how brazen is this operation one must realize what a strong spotlight Kefauver focused on the Newport-Covington area. He called it one of the major gambling centers in the United States; he stressed that every kind of gambling racket ran wide open there; he indicted the manner in which the Newport-Covington "layoff" moguls lured legitimate racetracks into collusion with the mob through the medium of what is known as "comeback" money. The term is simply explained. Big "layoff" operators, like bookies all up and down the chain, seek to protect their guaranteed edge. One way to do this is to send an agent to the track where a crucial race is being run to put $50,000 or even as much as $100,000 into the pari-mutuel machines. Such a heavy play whacks down the odds on a dangerous horse. If the nag wins, the bookies collect at the track, and pay off their losses at reduced odds. If he doesn't, they have at least balanced their books and insured their profit. This practice has led to active connivance between some so-called legitimate tracks and the mobs. The tracks woo mob money by offering commissions to mob brokers as an inducement to pour into the pari-mutuel machines the heavy cash that serves only to knock down the odds and in the end gyp bettors at the race tracks. Kefauver had excoriated this practice, but one would think he was shouting to a nation of deaf mutes, for after ten years nothing has changed except, perhaps, for the worse.

One of Kefauver's more fascinating discoveries dealt with the volume of "comeback" money that the Newport-Covington czars poured into pari-mutuel machines across the nation. A master of this maneuver, Kefauver found, was Louis (Rosy) Rosenbaum, of Newport, who handled a five-telephone "layoff" operation in a small office cuddled behind a high-sounding "front" name, the Northern Kentucky Hospitalization Insurance Agency. Even in 1947 and 1948, when Frank Erickson was still operating and the Newport-Covington sector had not yet become the nation's "layoff" capital, Rosenbaum had built up such a business that he had to pay income taxes of $200,000. A check of his phone records showed that he made 1,053 long-distance calls in a single month.

Rosenbaum kept busy two "comeback" agents, Fred Cogan and Richard Remer, making the circuit of the nation's race tracks to pour mob money into the pari-mutuel machines. Cogan testified that Rosenbaum paid him $150 a week to station himself at a telephone near a race track. Throughout the afternoon, he would keep in touch with Rosenbaum's Kentucky headquarters by calling collect, and on Rosenbaum's orders he would go into the track and bet the designated amount on the specified danger horse. Funds for this procedure were constantly replenished by fat money orders wired to Cogan by Western Union—a vivid illustration of the hard fact that, even at this level, betting is a losing proposition, with wins never making up for losses.

Rosenbaum's other agent, Remer, had a far more cushiony setup than Cogan at one track on his circuit—that at Bowie, Md. Here he had made special arrangements with track officials and was allowed to use a telephone in the track office. In addition, Bowie graciously permitted Remer to deposit a huge lump sum with its pari-mutuel clerk and to bet from this bankroll until it was depleted. Remer was just one of the commission agents or "comeback money men" operating at Bowie. A vivid idea of the tremendous amounts of money involved in the over-all "layoff" operation is conveyed by the Kefauver Committee testimony. Bowie is one of the nation's smaller tracks, with play by no means as huge and important as it is at larger racing centers; yet, in just one ten-day period, commission agents poured $500,000 into its pari-mutuel machines.

The Kefauver disclosures put a damper on activities in the Newport-Covington area for a time in the early 1950's; but by 1955 fear had subsided and the racketeers were running bigger and better supermarkets. In 1957,

The Reporter magazine, in an excellent article that obviously no one on any level of law enforcement ever saw, tried to call national attention to the flourishing Monte Carlo in northern Kentucky. Its author, James Maxwell, found the flossy gambling room of the Beverly Hills Country Club, just six miles from the heart of Cincinnati, running at a steady tempo, with two or three crap tables, a couple of roulette games, a chuck-a-luck session, and several blackjack games.

Other gambling dens were also running wide open, the bookmaking business was brisk, and wire rooms recorded and flashed the results from race tracks throughout the nation. Maxwell recorded one contretemps that seems to speak volumes about the real interests of the law. During the Kefauver probe in 1951, Newport Police Chief George Gugel had professed to be dumfounded when informed about the state of affairs in his own town. He had conceded he was "surprised" to be told of such wide-open gambling "because I've never been in there. All I know is what somebody told me." Some five years later it became rather embarrassingly apparent that the chief, in the interim, had acquired more personal knowledge. The *Louisville Courier-Journal* managed to inspire a Newport detective, Jack Thiem, to raid Glenn Schmidt's Playtorium. When Thiem crashed the place, he was astonished to find Chief Gugel and three brother detectives on the premises. The *Courier-Journal* photographer attempted to record this mutually surprising confrontation for posterity, but Chief Gugel ordered him arrested and had his film destroyed. The final outcome was particularly appropriate; for, though Americans persist in trying to ignore the brutal fact, the only man who ever gets harmed in such encounters is the innocent who tries to uphold the law. Chief Gugel, it is true, was suspended, but only temporarily. He was soon right back on the job. But Jack Thiem, the detective who had had the presumption to pull a gambling raid, wasn't so fortunate; he got fired.

In view of this result, it is hardly surprising to find that the Newport-Covington area is still the nerve center of the nation's big-league gambling. The New York Commission of Investigation's raids in late 1959 established that upstate New York bookies were funneling their top "layoff" play to both Biloxi and Covington, but principally to Covington. Eliot Lumbard, the commission's chief counsel, estimated that the Newport-Covington area provides "the basic insurance" for perhaps 90 per cent of the bookmaking activity in this country." Walsh added that the investigation had shown that Covington exercises important controls from the top. For example, he said, he found that Covington "assigns code numbers to upstate New York bookmakers." On one occasion, a New York bookie wanted to get his code number changed, but the Covington headquarters refused to accommodate him "until it could be checked with the boss."

When a bookie in upstate New York has nothing to say about the code number under which he operates, but has to wait for the approval of "the boss" in Covington to get it changed, the tight control that the underworld exercises over every phase of the bookmaking racket would seem amply demonstrated. This theme was developed in significant detail before the New York commission by the federal prober, Manners.

Manners and his staff had made an exceedingly thorough preliminary study of the nation's bookmaking. They had tracked underworld connections by studying literally thousands of telephone call slips and piecing together the pattern that emerged from these links crisscrossing the nation.

Manners put the picture in precise terms. He testified that the money not laid off at the tracks—in other words the colossal final take that is insured by "vigorish" and losing bets—"ends up in a top pool, top level of organized crime. This is the amazing feature of organized gambling. That two dollars [bet with the corner handbook] finally ends up in part throughout the nation either in Kentucky, in Biloxi or one or two other places in the West."

Manners explained that in analyzing the pattern of telephone contacts, his agents had spotted what seemed to be a highly significant circumstance. Repeatedly, after normal working hours and on off-days, calls would be placed to the "layoff" centers in Biloxi and Covington from phones of prominent gambling casino owners in Las Vegas and Havana. These calls were never made at times to interfere with the busy routine of working days, but after-hours connections were "many and frequent." Manners said he could only conclude, since federal investigators are barred from wiretapping and so could not listen in on these conversations, that:

"This is the checkup. This is to find out how much you have made today or how much are we doing this week. It's the same few who control everything. The same few are there because of all of us. I feel that gambling is the initial source of moneys. This is their [the underworld's] entire money that they can use for everything."

In this testimony Manners indicated the hidden ties that give top echelons of the underworld control over literally billions of dollars. The prestige and influence that such enormous wealth inevitably commands may be seen in the simple fact that the vast operations on which the bookmaking trade depends cannot be kept secret—yet still they flourish. Hirshfield's role in furnishing "the line," the key function of Biloxi and Covington in providing "the layoff" —the first two of bookmaking's essential three services— are completely open. Similarly obvious is the final step— the supplying of fast results from the track.

Speed in flashing the name of the winner of a race is essential to the bookie. In the first place, fast results stimulate "action." One of the axioms of the trade is that the quicker a bettor on the first race finds out how he fared, the quicker he can be lured to bet again. If he has won, he has money to gamble with; if he has lost—for in this the psychology works both ways—he may be tempted to double his bet the next time around in the futile scramble to "get even." Either way, the faster the bookie gets the news from the track, the faster this news gets to the bettor, the greater is going to be the volume of the bookie's business, the greater his take from the ever-mounting "vigorish."

Important as this motive is, there is a second that is even more vital to a bookie's welfare. This involves a racket within the racket known as "past-posting." Its genesis is simple. If a conniver can devise a method of getting results from a track faster than the bookie gets them, he can put a bet down fast on a horse that he knows has already won. Innumerable gimmicks have been figured out by unscrupulous souls to take the bread right out of the mouth of hard-working books in this fashion, and it is a sad fact of life that a bookie simply can't put any trust in his customers. He always has to keep alert and make certain that he gets the results from the tracks faster than anyone else can get them. This crucial need is most obligingly met by a father-son combination, Albert and Joseph Tollin, who operate the Delaware Sports Services from offices in a roadhouse-type building at 601 Tathall Street, Wilmington, Delaware.

Walsh, in the New York hearings, traced the development of the Tollin service. In the days before the Kefauver probe, the furnishing of race results was dominated by the Continental Wire Service, controlled by Al Capone's mob heirs in Chicago. At that time, the Tollins' Delaware Wire Service was a subscriber of Continental. When the Kefauver exposure drove Continental out of business, there was a scramble for the lush proceeds. Several competitors failed, but the Tollins' service survived. Every bit of information received by both Delaware and New York authorities indicates that this survival was probably the result of high underworld ties. "No one is letting Mr. Tollin carve up this lush melon which was Continental's plush list before," Walsh declared in his testimony before the New York commission. "Syndicate gambling controls this list just as it controls other things in professional gambling."

Just as Hirshfield supplies the initial need of the betting cycle by providing "the line" from Minneapolis, the Tollins wind it up by flashing "the results" from Wilmington. They serve, by their own admission, some 4,000 to 8,000 books all over the United States, in Canada, and even in Europe. They have an especially heavy clientele in the northeastern states, and New York probers identified a full fifty of their raided upstate books as Tollin customers. Like Hirshfield, like the "layoff" operations in Biloxi and Covington, the Tollins have a passion for code names and "client" anonymity. The standard procedure is for customers to contact the Tollins' by phone or Western Union and contract for their services. This initial contact establishes a code name like "Joe 13" by which the customer ever after will be known. The Tollins' fees range from $5 to $10 for a report on a single race up to $50 for a full day's coverage of the racing program.

Walsh and Detective Walter J. Wassmer, of the Delaware Attorney General's Office, described the Tollins' technique. The basic operation involves getting an instantaneous flash on the winner from inside the track. For this, the Tollins rely on what is known as "the pitcher-catcher" system. The "pitcher" is an agent who is stationed inside the track, right on top of the finish line. The "catcher" is spotted outside, with an open telephone line into the Tollin office in Delaware, ready to "catch" and relay the word from the "pitcher."

This word may be flashed visually, if the "pitcher" and "catcher" are stationed so that they have a clear view of each other; if this isn't possible, modern devices like the walkie-talkie may be used. If the contact is visual, the "pitcher" will wigwag a previously agreed signal to designate the winning horse, or he may merely hold up a card containing the number of the winner. The instant the signal is received, the "catcher" calls the name of the horse into the ear of either Albert or Joseph Tollin, waiting on the other end of the phone line in Wilmington, and the entire Tollin system swings into action.

The Tollin headquarters occupies two floors of the Tathall Street house. On the main floor is the business office; on the second floor, in a box of a room ten feet by twelve, is the result-flashing center. Here are a switchboard and a switchboard operator; in the center of the room, a table; and at the table, usually, Albert Tollin and a girl assistant. On the table are three curiously rigged wooden boxes. The boxes are plain wooden crates, about one-and-a-half feet square, padded with foam rubber. They are placed facing Albert Tollin. As race time nears and calls begin coming in, Tollin's girl assistant hangs the telephone receivers over the edge of these padded boxes, so that the mouthpieces are within the box.

"About two or three minutes before a race is run, why there is quite a calamity," Detective Wassmer told the New York commission. "The telephones are jumping and jingling. Tollin himself would be holding a telephone in one hand, one in the other. His girl on the other side will be taking telephone calls. The phones are just jingling."

When all the phone mouthpieces that can be accommodated have been placed in the sounding boxes, the switchboard girl puts a hold key on each of the other incoming calls. She draws the hold keys up in a line, and waits with a ruler in her hand. Tollin, on the open telephone line to his "catcher" outside the race track, gets the winner, shouts the name at the padded boxes. Instantly, all the bookie calls dangling in the boxes are taken care of. At the same time, the switchboard girl relays the winner's name to all those waiting on the first row of hold keys on her switchboard. With one sweep of her ruler, she flips off this line of keys, flips on a new batch. With incredible dispatch, the Tollins' frantic clientele receive their bread-and-butter information.

Telephone and Western Union records have clearly established the tremendous volume of the Tollins' business. Walsh estimated that the Tollins' Delaware Sports Service must chalk up a profit of at least $500,000 a year. There is no secret about it. But neither is anything being done about it. As in Minnesota with the Hirshfield operation, the local law in Delaware professes itself helpless. The Tollins, like Hirshfield, are keeping carefully within the bounds of local legality. Their activity, as Walsh pointed out, would perhaps have been impossible had Kefauver been able to secure the passage of a law he recommended to ban the rapid interstate transmission of race results. The proposal was attacked on the grounds that it might be an opening wedge in limiting the transmission of information and so curbing the freedom of the press, and for this reason Congress turned a deaf ear to Kefauver's plea and let the nation's bookmakers retain comfortable twilight zones of legality. Taking advantage of every loophole, the books have employed the decade since Kefauver to reap more billions than ever before. No one doubts that the list of Tollin customers, hiding behind their code numbers, would reveal virtually every major operator in the bookmaking racket—but nobody on any level of law enforcement is doing anything to pick up the clues.

"His list, even more than Hirshfield's, would break up the racket," Walsh said of Albert Tollin at the New York hearings.

Commissioner Jacob Grumet, who began his long career as an aide to Thomas E. Dewey in Dewey's racket-busting days, was frankly puzzled. "But it seems to me, if the authorities were alert," he said, "at least an attempt should be made to decipher the code and find out who these people are."

This is certainly elementary common sense, yet no one on any effective level of law enforcement seems astute enough to see the obvious. Milton Wessel and Joseph Manners tried; but almost as soon as Manners, having pieced together an intricate cross-continental pattern of telephone contacts, made his first move against the rackets in preliminary raids staged in the spring of 1959, the U.S. Attorney General's Special Unit on Organized Crime was disbanded and its personnel folded back into the old bureaus and divisions of the Department of Justice. Since that time, except for some minor raids by Internal Revenue agents in the spring of 1960, nothing of importance has happened.

In discussing this frustrating pattern of crime and official inaction with Milton Wessel, I summed up this picture and asked a question.

"Milton," I said, "this is what gets me. Here you have vital services running wide-open, known to everybody, using code names to hide the identity of their clients; and everybody pretends there is nothing they can do about it. Isn't it prima-facie evidence of conspiracy to commit a crime to run a business and deal with customers by using code names?"

"It is to me," Wessel said. "There is a vacuum in law enforcement. Here in this room [his hand swept a well-populated dining room in its gesture] you probably couldn't find a single man who either doesn't bet himself or know all about the betting that goes on. Everybody knows it. But nobody does anything about it. New laws might help, but the federal government now has all the authority it really needs, in my opinion at least, to move against the rackets. All that is needed is for somebody to *act.*"

Anyone want to bet (6 to 5, of course) that nobody will?

3

THE SWEEP OF CORRUPTION

IN a county seat in upstate New York, a criminal court case was almost ready to go to the jury. The judge called a recess before delivering his charge, and in the lull, the lawyer for the defendant strolled out into the corridor, nodding to acquaintances, joking with friends—and occasionally pocketing money. For the lawyer was a bookmaker, and his place of business on this particular day was in the very halls of the courthouse!

While doing a brisk business in illegal bets, the lawyer-bookmaker spotted an acquaintance and competitor, another bookie. They greeted each other, and standing there in the so-called hall of justice, they discussed the irony of the situation.

"What a laugh this is!" said the lawyer-bookmaker. "Here I am, in the midst of trying a criminal case, and while I'm waiting for the judge to get his instructions to be read to the jury, I'm out here taking bets."

The two laughed. Then the single-profession bookmaker asked the lawyer-bookmaker: "Well, is it hard to get convicted for bookmaking?"

The lawyer chuckled and said: "Don't worry about it,

they will never convict you. Just be careful. Don't let them see any records." After reflecting a moment, he added, "Well, even if you are caught, there is really no worry. They once did send some guys to jail here, but the case wound up getting thrown out of court anyhow."

New York investigators, listening in on a wiretapped phone, heard the lawyer-bookie chuckle as he related this encounter to an acquaintance that same night. Later William Walsh recounted the story at Commission of Investigation hearings in the spring of 1960. The commissioners, themselves lawyers, were plainly shocked. "You mean," one of them asked Walsh, "that this lawyer was actually also a bookmaker?" Walsh assured the commission that this was indeed the case and that the lawyer had been arrested subsequently for bookmaking. The idea that a lawyer—"a representative of the court"—should not only be a bookmaker but should ply his trade in the very courthouse represented, Walsh said, the most shocking single example of complete *contempt* for the law that was uncovered in the New York probe.

It was not, however, the only example. Anyone concerned about the state of our society will find ample justification for that concern in the prevailing attitudes Walsh's investigators found in New York. Bookies seemed almost to spit upon the law. "In fully half a dozen towns," Walsh says, "we listened in on bookies chatting with each other about the cops. Time and again the same phrases would be repeated. Their favorite expression of contempt for the police was 'the little men' or 'the little men in blue.' We heard those phrases almost everywhere we went, and they were spoken in a way that registered absolute and complete contempt."

The New York investigation, which was to produce the

clearest view of big-league gambling since the revelations of the Kefauver committee, grew out of the discovery of a nasty mess in the college city of Ithaca, home of Cornell University. Here football pools had become such a huge racket that discarded betting slips could be found cluttering the streets all around the Cornell campus after a big weekend. The city of Ithaca itself is the county seat of Tompkins County; it contains a number of industrial plants and is the shopping center for surrounding farm districts. Its normal population is about 29,000, which is swollen to 40,000 when Cornell is in session. Normally, one might expect that a small college city of this size would be cleaner than most but the New York commission found that every kind of gambling racket was running openly in Ithaca—and that the total gambling handle in this not-so-quiet college city was a quarter of a million dollars annually.

The Ithaca probe was touched off by complaints lodged with Inspector John J. Quinn, in command of the Criminal Intelligence Unit of the State Police. Quinn consulted with the Commission of Investigation and in the early fall of 1958 sent two troopers into Ithaca for a preliminary checkup. The detectives went directly to addresses that had been mentioned in the complaints as gambling centers. They paid their first visit to the Varsity Billiards parlor at 107 North Tioga Street, less than seventy-five yards from police headquarters. In the billiard room they found a cashier's booth in which was a desk stacked high with football slips. The proprietor, Louis (Murphy) Chelekis, and two helpers in the booth were constantly busy. The phone rang continuously; bettors kept coming in and walking up to the booth to get their money down on a horse. Chelekis and his aides accommodated all comers, booking horse races and writing numbers slips. Observing all this, the two detectives strolled up to the booth and placed bets with Chelekis. Thus, with no more effort than it took to walk in from the street, did the two detectives confirm the reality of wide-open gambling in Ithaca.

From the Varsity Billiards parlor they went to a second address, 124 South Aurora Street. Once more their advance information turned out to be good. The address was a "policy drop," visited each day by eight or nine numbers "runners." The troopers had no trouble striking up an acquaintance on the sidewalk and placing a numbers bet with one of them. This runner turned out to be an eager pitchman for the mob. He assured the detectives that "the fellows from the Varsity" were runing a big-money dice game in the Sons of Italy Lodge at 417 State Street every Sunday night, and each day there was also a card game at the lodge with "plenty of action." If the visitors wanted excitement, said the numbers runner, they ought to get in on the game, and he obligingly gave them the name of a sponsor who could get them into this fraternal fun house. A little investigation showed that the windows of the lodge hall were little more than an arm's length away from the side wall of the Ithaca Theatre, operated by Mayor John F. Ryan. The lodge had been erected in 1949, and, ever since, one of its main sources of income had been the revenue derived from gambling—originally from slot machines and a house cut on poker and blackjack games, and later, beginning in May, 1958, from a cut on dice games that lured a play of from $30,000 to $40,000 a night.

The detectives, following up the leads that had fallen into their laps, wangled their way into the Sons of Italy Lodge. In the gambling room upstairs over the bar, they found about twenty men gathered around a felt-covered dice table. Individual wagers as high as $100 were frequent, and $500 bets were not uncommon. The playing clientele was quite obviously a rough crowd, drawn—as subsequent investigation showed—from racket havens throughout central New York and northern Pennsylvania.

Before state probers could follow up this preliminary inquiry, Cornell University officials forced a semblance of local action. On November 5, 1958, the university protested officially to the Ithaca Police Department that large quantities of football slips were inundating the Cornell campus and adjacent areas. Confronted with this challenge, the local police, who hadn't made a single gambling arrest in three years, swung into action. Sergeant Cornelius, who headed the detectives working under the tight, personal control of Police Chief Herbert L. Van Ostrand, went to work with utmost simplicity. He just walked the seventy-five yards that separated police headquarters and the Varsity Billiards parlor. As he entered he saw a man in the betting booth writing out a policy numbers slip and another taking a bet on a horse race. Though the detective sergeant was naturally well known to the gamblers, they paid not the slightest attention to him. This was too much for Cornelius. He stepped forward and arrested one of the men in the booth. As he was about to leave with his prisoner, Louis Chelekis walked in. The detective asked Chelekis if he was the proprietor and if he permitted his employees to take bets. When Chelekis answered, "Sure," to both questions, he got the surprise of his life. Cornelius arrested him.

In the days that followed, there was a considerable flurry of police activity. Eight naughty gamblers were arrested, a figure that might look fairly impressive in a city of Ithaca's size unless one was aware, as the New York commission was, that at least forty to fifty professionals were steadily plying their trade there. Furthermore, no action was taken to interfere with the $30,000 to $40,000 Sunday night dice game that was running in the lodge hall just a few feet from the mayor's theater.

Confronted with a brushup instead of a cleanup, the New York commission acted. At 10 A.M. on February 15, 1959, its agents and a squad of State Police raided the Sons of Italy Lodge, arrested twenty-eight men and seized $15,-000 in gambling cash.

Indicative of the kind of characters that large-scale gambling breeds were the dossiers of some of the prisoners. Fourteen of them had a cumulative record of forty-two convictions for lawbreaking in at least nine cities of the state. The convictions were such offenses as abduction, burglary, carrying a dangerous weapon, disorderly conduct, gambling, grand larceny, illegal possession of firearms, impersonating an officer, leaving the scene of an accident, malicious mischief, transportation of females for prostitution—in other words, nearly the gamut of crime. This was the kind of human trash that had been given the keys to the city of Ithaca under the eyes of a complaisant police force.

No satisfactory explanation for this immunity was ever obtained by the New York commission. They held private hearings on the state of affairs in Ithaca and found no real evidence of corruption. Yet the lax conditions that existed in the city were those that are almost invariably associated with corruption. The gambling rackets had remained undisturbed for so long that they had acquired status; they were practically a community institution. Abundant testimony showed that average citizens knew in detail about the gambling that ran wide open under their noses; that the local police had had many accurate reports about them but had never acted; that many of these reports, filed personally with Chief Van Ostrand, had vanished mysteriously right out of the department's files.

Mayor Ryan gave testimony characterized by admitted knowledge and unexplained lassitude. He admitted that he knew about the big dice games because "a lot of out-of-town men [were] going by my theater every Sunday afternoon"; that he knew about the horse betting and numbers play; that he had "heard" football pool tickets were being freely circulated throughout the city and the college area. The Mayor conceded that Chief Van Ostrand "probably" had not done a good job; he "supposed" he wouldn't be able to put complete confidence in the Chief's competence in the future; he "probably" would tell the Chief that he would have to do better; he wasn't "sure" whether these "probable" instructions would have any more effect in the future than in the past; and yes, there had "probably" been a time when he realized that the Chief wasn't exactly doing his job, but he, the Mayor, hadn't insisted on a cleanup.

Q. Why did you not at that time lay down the law to him [the police chief] that he had to stop that game?

A. I don't know. I just didn't do anything about it. That's all.

Sergeant Cornelius explained that there was "a local ground rule" to leave gamblers alone unless someone filed "a specific complaint." In this unfortunate eventuality, the matter would be discussed with the District Attorney to see if it was absolutely necessary to do anything about it. Cornelius phrased it this way:

"I don't think it is probably right . . . I can see that now. Before—I have been brought up here for seventeen years, where you never acted on gambling or a raid or anything without going to the Chief of Police, and in turn you might be called for a conference where you knew the District Attorney was going to be let in on it. You never acted without consulting the District Attorney on any of these things, and if he sees fit to knock off some place, you knock them off. If not, it was either dropped or negated or whatever you want to call it."

The secret understanding that Louis Chelekis and his ring had with someone somewhere was no secret to members of the police force. They had plenty of experience with the influence of Ithaca's "Mr. Untouchable." One police officer testified: "I've been on here approximately thirteen years. I remember once about seven years ago—shortly after I was on there, one fellow made a raid on a place in the city. He received ten days [suspension] because it wasn't an authorized raid." This was hardly the kind of reward calculated to inspire other policemen to do their duty. The impression of the force as a whole was summed up in this testimony by another patrolman: "I talked this over with the officers there. I can't recall exactly who it was now, but they stated that the Chief and everybody knows about it. If he wants to do anything, he'd do it. There is no sense in me sticking my neck out because he'd blackball me. . . ."

While Chief Van Ostrand had inherited this situation when he became head of the department, he had done nothing to correct it. Indeed, there was every indication that, under him, morale became worse. Testimony showed that he had been told one of his policemen was actually frequenting the card game at the Sons of Italy Lodge, but he didn't even question the offender about his conduct. On two occasions in the summer of 1958 a patrolman making his rounds found the rear door of the lodge unlocked, walked in, and observed the gambling game in action. The reports he filed with the Chief disappeared. In September, 1958, two other members of the department walked in on the gambling game, were shocked at the size of the play they saw, and hurried out to the Chief's home to inform him of what was going on. "I told him that we could go down," one of the officers testified. "He said, 'No, we may not get anything. They may be gone. We may not hit anything. There may not be any gambling at all.' "

In November, 1958, still another member of the department walked in on the high-stakes game, observed the play, and the next morning reported to the Chief. This sequence from the commission's transcript tells what happened:

A. I walk in. I said, "Herb, such and such is going on. Maybe it's little, maybe it isn't. I don't know. But there's money laying all over the place. There's people down there that I don't know. I haven't seen them."

Q. What did he say to that?

A. He said, "We know there's something going on down there. If you will give me a notarized statement, I'll put it on file." Those are his exact words. "If you will give me a notarized statement, I'll put it on file."

What happened to such reports was described by other officers, who said they "just seemed to disappear." One policeman testified:

"I know there were several complaints made out concerning gambling in this vicinity, but nothing was ever recorded there, and complaints just seemed to disappear."

Q. What do you mean by "disappear"?

A. Well, they were put under the Chief's door, let's put it that way, and after that nobody ever saw hide nor hair of them.

This situation bred such disgust in the working echelons of the department that, as one member testified, a lot of the men "were about ready to turn their badges in."

As a result of the Ithaca probe, several things happened. Murphy Chelekis pleaded guilty to gaming charges, but received considerate treatment—a suspended sentence and a year's probation. Mayor Ryan was defeated when he ran for re-election, but Chief Van Ostrand remained as police chief. The exposure to which his department had been subjected caused some changes in Van Ostrand's attitude; the drive on gambling became top police business in Ithaca, and Chief Van Ostrand hastily adopted recommendations made by the commission for the improvement of the department. The commission in its report could only hope that these changes would prove permanent.

Enough had been uncovered in Ithaca to show that organized gambling was rampant in both upstate cities and rural areas. The Ithaca gamblers had been linked to others in the underworld all across central New York, in Pennsylvania, and in Canada. Obviously, they represented only one segment of a massive illegal operation. And so, at the urging of Bill Walsh and Eliot Lumbard, the New York commission decided to undertake a state-wide investigation.

Months were devoted to careful preparation. The commission's agents and State Police worked on the investigation from May to late October, 1959, and during the last four months Inspector Quinn devoted almost his entire fifty-man detective force to the probe. Many leads were developed through wiretapping, a legal procedure in New York providing authorities first obtain a court order.

Eliot Lumbard stresses that the raids, and the vivid insight the investigation furnished into the mechanics of the gambling racket, would have been impossible except for the New York law that permits wiretapping.

"I want to make this absolutely clear," Lumbard says. "A lot of objections have been voiced to wiretapping, but this is a case that could never have been developed without it. The telephone is, of course, the bookie's principal instrument, the means by which he transacts the great amount of his business. If the law didn't have the right to wiretap, it would be almost the same as granting the bookies a blanket immunity. We built this case, we pieced together the links and relationship between one bookie and another by wiretapping. In our view, to forbid wiretapping is just like tying the hands of the law behind its back."

For more than four months, commission and State Police detectives monitored scores of wiretaps. The tap on one bookie's line would disclose his contacts with others; these led to new taps and new discoveries in an ever-widening circle. Walsh, who directed the field work, accepted the risk that, by delay, some suspects might be lost. Actually, during the months of eavesdropping, some twenty books moved their locations or went underground for one reason or another; but the loss was more than made up for by the piecing together of a huge cross-state network.

By October, 1959, the commission had amassed evidence against one hundred books operating in twenty-seven cities and towns in seventeen counties. The chain ran from Fort Edward and Saratoga Springs on the east through the Troy-Albany-Schenectady area; then west, through Amsterdam, Johnstown, Frankfort, Rome and Syracuse; from Syracuse through Solvay, Auburn, and Geneva to Rochester; and from Rochester west into the Buffalo area, including towns like Tonawanda and North Tonawanda, Lewiston, Lockport, and Niagara Falls. To raid such a sweep of territory, extending from the Hudson River to Lake Erie, was a master undertaking. Several hundred policemen were marshaled for the striking force. Complete secrecy was maintained until the last moment; then the individual raiding squads were organized and briefed, and at exactly 3 P.M., October 23, 1959, a busy Friday afternoon, the raiders struck one hundred books scattered across the state and, in addition, four policy banks in Buffalo.

So complete was the surprise that the bookmakers and policy writers were caught, in the words of the commission's subsequent report, "as they were busily employed in transacting the day's play. . . . A mountain of evidence was seized. Voluminous books, records and papers maintained by the bookmakers in keeping their accounts were found. Punchboards, policy slips, special dice and cards, football and baseball pool slips, horse-parlay books and other miscellaneous gambling paraphernalia were among the materials seized. Other equipment, such as adding machines, powerful short-wave radio and ticker tapes, were taken. Guns were discovered on three premises. So great was the amount of material that it required six weeks for Commission accountants and agents and the State Police, assisted by three bookmaking and policy experts graciously loaned by the New York City Police Department, to catalogue and evaluate these items for their evidentiary worth."

The need for precise timing and perfect execution was illustrated vividly by the speed with which word of the raids bounced around in gambling circles.

"In one instance, in about fifteen minutes," Walsh reported "the troopers who were at that time sorting out the evidence seized, received a call from Florida over the bookmaker's phone, warning the bookmaker that there were raids going on in that area, for him to look out and close up for the day. Unfortunately for him, it was fifteen minutes too late."

When the mass of evidence was finally evaluated, the commission felt that it had obtained as detailed and accurate a view of bookmaking as it was possible to get. The seized ledgers of the bookies, for example, established beyond all doubt the relative importance of various phases of gambling play. This analysis showed graphically how important sporting events, in addition to horse racing, have become in the business of the bookmaker. For the bookies' total play divided this way: horse racing, 42 per cent; baseball, 30 per cent; basketball, 15 per cent; football, 12 per cent (not including football pools in which virtually every bookie dealt); and boxing and miscellaneous other items, 1 per cent.

Walsh concedes that, for several reasons, this breakdown is not definitive. He points out that the raids were made in late October when the baseball season was finished and the college basketball season had not yet begun. The commission, in evaluating its figures, also figured in baseball play based on estimates picked up on wiretaps during the summer, but evidence on the size of this play was obviously incomplete. The commission did not even attempt to assess the play on baseball, football, and basketball pools, all of which flourish with an extremely high percentage of profit to the promoter—ranging up to a colossal 92 per cent on a widely distributed pool.

"Our figures reflect only what we can mathematically prove," Walsh says. But he adds that there is no doubt that, if the total sports play could be tabulated, the relative importance of horse racing in a bookie's gross would be reduced drastically. He calculates that horse racing might drop to only 30 to 35 per cent of the total, an opinion in general agreement with Wessel's estimate assigning both baseball and football heavier wagering totals than the races.

One of the great fascinations of the New York probes lies in the revelation of the essential dishonesty of the gambling rackets. The delusion that the professional gambler is a gentleman lawbreaker quickly evaporates in the face of the evidence: gambling is a dirty business, run by crooks who have no intention of giving the sucker a chance. From the standpoint of the operators, the very term "gambling" is a misnomer; there is no gamble in gambling from their vantage point, there is only the remorseless reaming of fools who are deluded into believing they have a chance.

You hear much talk about "honest houses" and "honest percentages," but the New York probe showed that these games are almost always rigged. The mechanics of such rigging were vividly illustrated in a seizure made during the raids. In one bookie establishment, the raiders found an eighty-page catalogue, distributed by a Chicago firm that has evidently built a profitable business out of manufacturing crooked devices to help gamblers fleece the suckers. The manufacturer, of course, disclaimed any intent "to perpetrate a fraud," but then went on to describe just how handy his devices would be to a man with unbridled larceny in his heart.

Advertisements in the catalogue described the virtues of crooked dice, loaded dice, dice that have particular points that will come up more frequently than others, card spreaders, card holdouts, marked decks, and contact lenses for reading marked cards. The rigged dice sold from $10 to $30 a set. "We cannot recommend these dice too highly for taking care of dangerous front-line play," the catalogue proclaimed, describing the virtues of a particular set. Of another, it boasted: "These dice will stand close inspection and get by in fast company." Of still another: "This set will give the banker or fader a very strong percentage, no switching. . . ." The firm also highly recommended a device that could be attached to the lower part of the coat, where it held and concealed a pair of loaded dice until a crucial moment. "Lower your hand and, presto, like magic, you have switched another pair of dice into your hand. It takes very little practice to be an expert switcher in a few minutes," the catalogue assured its customers.

Cards were rigged with equal ingenuity. The manufacturer's catalogue described and illustrated "contact lens cards that cannot be seen with the naked eye." The cards look like any legitimate, unmarked deck but once special contact lenses have been affixed to the eye, hidden symbols on the back of each card spring to life, and it becomes as easy to read an opponent's hand from the back as it is for him to read it from the front. The value of such magic lenses to the sharpie is indicated by the fact that the Chicago manufacturer was advertising "new improved triple contact lenses" at $160 a pair.

When a firm can afford to issue an eighty-page catalogue devoted exclusively to rigged devices, and when it disseminates this nationally, it is obvious that it must be doing a tremendous business. It can only do such a business if the gambling games of America are crooked on a vast scale. The New York raiders were not crashing gambling casinos, but bookmaking headquarters. Even so, in some half-dozen instances, they picked up as a by-product of their raids rigged dice and contact lens cards like those advertised. And Francis S. McGarvey, Superintendent of New York State Police, in subsequent testimony before the New York commission testified that rigging of gambling games was an almost common experence. His troopers in their raids, McGarvey said, frequently found "that the dice were crooked, and we also found roulette wheels of establishments that were wired up and, in some instances, the crap tables were magnetized."

Yet the scum who operate such crooked games are those with whom, through the distribution of an estimated $4.5 billion a year in graft, the politicians and the police of America are in partnership. The stench of the partnership reeks in many phases of American life, and in the course of the New York probe, investigators time and again came across its traces.

One strong trail was provided by telephone conversations overheard by detectives in areas where, through some incalculable upsurge of civic virtue, the bookmaking profession was under a cloud of temporary menace. In one upstate city, relations had been extremely cordial with the police department until, through a shift in city government, a new police commissioner was appointed. Suspicious of the lackadaisical performance of the police chief, the commissioner picked out a bright and energetic young detective lieutenant and formed his own gambling squad. This threat of competition stirred up the old order in the department. Grabbing the first evidence that came to hand, the "regulars" quickly made themselves a record by knocking off fourteen books. They then proudly put up a sign on the headquarters bulletin board, reading: "Fourteen for us, nothing for new squad." This show of vigor, however, turned out to be farcical in more respects than one. The cases against the fourteen raided books had been so hastily and sloppily prepared that all of them "went out the window" when they came to trial. The bookies themselves voiced the basic reality of the situation in succinct comments over their telephones. "It's these new guys who are killing us," they moaned. "They're causing all the trouble. We gotta do something about those old guys; we've been paying them too much."

In Syracuse, following the exposés of the Syracuse *Herald-Journal,* bookies communed over their tapped phones about the misery of their plight. The small-fry were in a flap. In one recorded conversation, two of these lower-echelon lice discussed the outlook. "There's too much heat on. We gotta get out of business," one said. "Yeah," the other agreed, "but we gotta go together. They'll knock us off because the big guys are protected."

The hoofprints of the "big guys" also showed like dinosaur's tracks throughout the New York probe. Nowhere did they show more clearly than in the activities of two important racketeer middlemen—Joseph Vizzi in Buffalo and Samuel Silver in Syracuse.

Vizzi was one of the craftiest operators New York detectives encountered. Bill Walsh's investigators were introduced to him when some of his calls began to come in over tapped wires. Even with the taps, however, it wasn't easy to tell just who Vizzi was or where he was calling from. For Vizzi would phone an associate collect, and in giving the number from which he was making the collect call, he would falsify the last couple of digits. For example, if the phone he was using ended in a number like 2300, Vizzi would say he was calling from "2301" or "2310." When investigators chased to sites where such phones were registered, they found themselves walking into beauty parlors, real estate offices, and other legitimate businesses far removed from the illicit business of Joe Vizzi. "It drove us crazy," Walsh says, "until we finally caught on to what he was doing."

Another of Vizzi's favorite stunts was his use of a telephone credit card. In placing calls, he would frequently give a credit card number, but it was never his own. He and some of his more sophisticated upstate associates had persuaded obliging friends to let them place calls, using the friends' numbers. The calls would then be charged to the credit card number given to the operator, frequently one belonging to an innocent dupe living miles away from the actual scene of operations. Whenever detectives tried to piece together a pattern from these telephone calls, they would find no calls, no clues leading back to Joe Vizzi.

Once Walsh's detectives had found their way through the maze of Vizzi's dissmulations, however, they kept close taps on him and listened while he instructed his less knowledgeable partners in the fine points of the bookie's art—like keeping all records on "flash paper." This is chemically treated paper that, at the faintest flick of flame, disintegrates in a puff of smoke.

"If you hold a piece at arm's length and touch a cigarette to it and let it drop, it will vanish before it hits the floor," Bill Walsh explains. "It practically explodes in air. There isn't even any ash left to speak of."

When New York raiders finally crashed Joe Vizzi's door, he gave them a vivid demonstration of the virtues of "flash paper." They found him sitting by a wastebasket from which a few wisps of smoke curled lazily. In the bottom was just the faintest trace of ash—all that was left of the records on which Joe Vizzi had recorded his bookmaking transactions.

Those records, had detectives been able to seize them intact, undoubtedly would have provided important clues to the top-level operations of the bookmaking syndicate. For Joe Vizzi's ties to the top hierarchy were betrayed in one telephone call that, despite his excessive caution, he had been incautious enough to make. This had been a call to one of the largest operators in bookmaking today—Al Mones in Miami.

"What you got?" Vizzi asked Mones.

Mones read off a string of horses, with the amounts of the bets on each. Vizzi took down the list. Then, as soon as he had finished his call to Mones, he telephoned a contact in Canada and read off the same list of horses and bets. It was obvious that Vizzi in Buffalo was acting as a go-between for Al Mones in Florida, relaying a heavy betting load to a "layoff" center in Canada. This was one link in the chain of operations of a huge gambling syndicate—how significant a link New York investigators were not to realize until much later.

Many of the contacts revealed in the investigation of Joseph Vizzi reappeared in that of Samuel Silver, a professional gambler from Syracuse. Silver insisted that he was currently a man without a blemish, although he admitted that in a less circumspect past he had bankrolled crap games and handled some "layoff" business. He, like Vizzi, was well acquainted with Al Mones in Florida and with Harry Ship, the "layoff" mogul of Montreal and the partner, according to the New York commission, of one of the most sinister figures in modern American gangdom—Carmine Galente.

Silver, despite what might be described as bashful reluctance, told a far-ranging story that embraced a wide variety of contacts. One name that he dropped was enough to make headlines. It was the name of Joseph Farbo, a lawyer and Vice Mayor of Rochester. Silver disclosed that, in 1946 or 1947, he had loaned Farbo $50,000 so that Farbo could purchase a couple of apartment houses. He gave the money to Farbo in cash, he said; no papers were signed, no interest was specified. Silver claimed also that the money had been repaid with interest, although here again there was no record of it.

Subsequently, between 1948 and 1951, Silver testified, he began to funnel money in large amounts into the stock of the Arizona Harness Racing Association. In all, he turned over $158,292 to Farbo to invest for him. Commissioner Grumet demanded whether Farbo was "fronting" for Silver in this deal, and Silver said: "You can call it that if you wish." He explained that he had thought it better to register his stock in Farbo's name because "We kind of thought that we would have difficulty in obtaining a license, which we did."

In Rochester, Vice Mayor Farbo explained that Silver had been "a client and friend" of his of long standing, and his only connection with the track deal, he said, had been to "act as nominee" for Silver.

Trying to trace the varied activities of the Vice Mayor's old friend proved difficult because Silver was a man who all his life had had an antipathy to committing facts to paper. He admitted he had never bothered to keep records. He admitted, too, that he had never bothered to pay as much as a penny in federal income taxes until 1953, when Uncle Sam finally awoke to this oversight and began to ask questions. The result, Silver acknowledged, was that he and his wife had been convicted of federal income tax evasion, and he had had to pony up $166,987.22 in taxes and penalties for the years from 1944 to 1957.

The questioning switched to Silver's acquaintances among the elite of the gambling fraternity, and it quickly developed that these were wide indeed. In addition to Al Mones in Florida, Silver admitted that he "very probably" had telephone contacts with "P. J." in Biloxi; that he was often in touch with a Chicago bookie whom he identified only as "Lefty" and to whom, he said, he identified himself by saying, "This is 160 calling"; and that he often made calls to Harry Ship in Montreal at HU 6-6996. But when Eliot Lumbard brought the name of Carmine Galente into the questioning, Silver quickly shied away.

Q. You know Harry Ship to be a partner of Carmine Galente?

A. I don't know about Carmine Galente.

Q. You never heard the name?

A. No.

Parenthetically, it should be noted that, if Silver never heard of the name of Carmine Galente, his is an ignorance virtually unique among the smart set along the fringes of the underworld. For Federal Bureau of Narcotics agents repeatedly have focused a strong public spotlight on the notorious Galente. He was the principal suspect in the 1943 murder of Carlo Tresca, the militant anti-Fascist publisher of an Italian-language newspaper in New York. A foe of Mussolini, Tresca was believed to have been marked for murder by the Italian dictator, operating through the American underworld, and strong suspicion focused upon Galente, who was held in prison for eight months before the case against him collapsed for lack of proof. In his long career, Galente has amassed a record of sixteen arrests, including one on suspicion of killing a policeman, and he served one twelve-and-a-half-year term for shooting a detective and two children during a holdup. Federal narcotics agents in recent years have traced his steady climb in power and influence to a top niche in today's syndicate hierarchy—a spot they often compare to that once held by Albert Anastasia.

Gambling and narcotics are the principal ingredients in the success story of Galente. In testimony before the New York commission, Henry Giordano, deputy commissioner of the Federal Narcotics Bureau, explained that the Kefauver disclosures in 1951 sent Galente and other American gamblers to seek sanctuary north of the border in Montreal. There Galente, Giordano testified, "lost no time in taking over control of gambling and other criminal pursuits in Montreal," cutting quite a swath until Royal Canadian Mounted Police caught up with him and shipped him back to the States. Here Galente played a prominent role in Vito Genovese's narcotics combine. He was among those indicted with Genovese, but he managed to stay on the lam long enough to avoid the trial that resulted in Genovese's conviction. Meanwhile, in Montreal, the "lay-off" headquarters in which Galente had had such a heavy interest continued to flourish under the direction of Harry Ship, and its ties stretched all the way to Cuba, ultimately involving Syracuse's Samuel Silver as a go-between.

Only some four or five months before the New York hearings in the spring of 1960, Silver agreed to act as Ship's agent in an intricate bit of international intrigue. Only pieces of the story were spread tantalizingly on the record; the rest is still hidden behind a screen of secrecy erected by top-level federal agencies that still have it under investigation. In general terms, the negotiations involved, on the one hand, the possibility of converting some $22 million in outlawed Cuban money into usable American cash and, on the other, the ability of the underworld to smuggle war munitions, including machine guns and tanks, into Cuba.

The money end of the eventually abortive transaction involved, according to the New York commission, a huge hoard amassed by the Eastern gambling syndicate in the

Havana gambling casinos that Meyer Lansky had established with the blessing of Cuban dictator Fulgencio Batista. When Fidel Castro threw out Batista and seized power, he abolished certain large-denomination bills—an action that made it impossible for the mob to use its hoarded cash unless a way could be found through the underworld black market, with its ties in Cuba, to turn the frozen bills into negotiable currency. This was the point at which Silver entered the picture. Acting on instructions from Ship, he testified, he went to the George Washington Hotel in New York City to meet a mysterious "Mr. Pryor" and try to arrange a deal to dispose of the hot Cuban money at a rate of 12 or 13 cents on the dollar. The cautious "Mr. Pryor," however, insisted on fingering some samples of the syndicate's spoiling Cuban treasure, and when Ship in Montreal balked at supplying samples, the whole deal fell through.

Such are the ramifications, literally international in scope, one stumbles upon when one tries to trace what happens to the flock of $2 bets placed with the corner handbooks. The reality collides with the myth that the American public so long has swallowed. The racing interests, the sporting interests, and last but not least the racket interests have all done their best to foster the belief that a little gambling, though technically illegal, is essentially innocent. In this they have succeeded. The general public reaction to bookmaking has been one, if not of outright support, at least of apathy. Bill Walsh has described it succinctly:

". . . People are simply confused or lulled into the belief that gambling is a simple, harmless pastime," he said. "When it is conducted on this type of scale, it is long gone from a harmless pastime."

How "long gone" was illustrated in an account of plot and murder related from the witness stand by Attorney General Edward J. McCormack, of Massachusetts. He described what he called a "Little Apalachin" conference held by mob delegates in Worcester, Mass., on December 8, 1959. Fifteen rooms in a Worcester hotel were rented for the night, and though McCormack used the term "little" in describing the meeting, it actually was a much larger meeting than the interrupted Apalachin conference two years earlier. There were 150 delegates from the northeastern states. None of the beds in the fifteen rented rooms were slept in; the hotel bill came to more than $600; and telephone traffic between Worcester and New York was heavy during the night-long discussions. Significantly, the crime conference was called just ten days before Milton Wessel succeeded in convicting twenty of the Apalachin mobsters in New York Federal Court, and it may well have been that the Eastern syndicate called the Worcester parley to straighten out tangled chains of command and replace key powers who were about to be deactivated by the law.

In any event, the decisions reached at Worcester quickly became apparent. Just fifteen days later, at 1:30 A.M., December 23, 1959, Gaetano Joseph DiNicola, alias Kiki Cuyler, the reputed gambling overlord of Hartford, was dispatched by five bullets while sitting in his car parked on a street in Connecticut's capital city. The underworld grapevine hinted that his execution was a reprisal for executive failure. The previous September 15, Connecticut State Police had raided thirty-four gambling joints, a damaging blow of the type that an efficient syndicate leader is supposed to know how to avoid. And DiNicola was also a man with ties and obligations elsewhere. Inspector Quinn of the New York State Police and McCormack both hinted that his murder might be traced back to New York. As Quinn put it, DiNicola was "definitely linked . . . with a very prominent gambler and racketeer in the State of New York."

The murder of DiNicola was followed by two others that seemed to stem from decisions reached at Worcester. On April 11, 1960, Edward Rothstein, of Newton, Massachusetts, a gambler and loan shark, with ties to both Boston and New York, was efficiently ventilated and stuffed into the trunk of his own car. And out in Youngstown, Ohio, a man known as S. Joseph, alias Sandy Naples, 50, reputedly the number two policy man in Youngstown, with close ties to the New York gambling mob, went walking up the steps of his girl friend's house and exposed his back to a volley of fatal bullets.

There is a definite war in our society between two systems of enforcement: the rule of law and the rule imposed by the guns of the underworld. Time and again the terrorism of the lawless has proved superior to the justice set up by society. The lips of potential witnesses are buttoned. In cases involving major gang lords, key witnesses are often simply erased; hardly ever is any gangland murder solved. This is the rule of terror, this the law of the gun that backs up the multi-billion dollar gambling rackets of America; and the chain, from corner handbook to the pinnacle of syndicate power, was clearly delineated in the New York probe. In the face of such evidence it becomes pertinent to inquire how the courts of New York State performed following the most perfectly executed raids ever launched against the state's bookmakers. The answer is, unfortunately, that they performed very badly.

Punishment was imposed so gently and considerately

that the courts gave the impression they were dealing with men seized in a street-corner scuffle. By April, 1960, when the New York commission held its public hearings, the judicial attitude had become glaringly apparent. By that time, fifty-two cases had been disposed of—fifty-one on guilty pleas, one by dismissal. Of the guilty, forty-one were "punished" by fines ranging from $5 to $500 and totaling a mere $11,690; five had fines or jail sentences actually suspended, suffering not even a slap on the wrist; and three were still awaiting sentence.

"Only two men actually went to jail; and those two, for thirty days . . . ," Walsh declared. "In many instances, those bookmakers had long and extensive criminal records, ranging from murder [to] narcotics and white-slaving. Despite these criminal records, they received only minimal fines."

It goes without saying that the average citizen would be punished more severely if he were convicted of speeding or littering the highway. It is customary to excuse the judiciary for its leniency by saying that the importance of the gambling issue is not properly understood. If it is ignorance, however, there should be even less excuse for it in the future. Bill Walsh, among others, went to considerable pains to put the issue squarely into focus during the New York hearings. He emphasized that the gambler in Syracuse who had victimized the $7,000-a-year wage-earner was later arrested for the fifth time—and for the fifth time he escaped with a small fine. Gamblers, Walsh said, shrug off fines, and look upon them as nothing more than a license fee that they would have to pay if they were legitimate businessmen. Indeed, the gambler often gets off more lightly than the businessman. A liquor license costs a lot more, for example, than most bookmakers pay in fines when, belatedly, the law catches up with them. Walsh cited the case of one bookie who had been fined eight times for gambling offenses. On his eighth conviction, he was fined only $125; over a period of years, his eight fines totaled a mere $400.

It is little wonder that when judges on the bench take such a tolerant attitude toward some of the foulest scum in America, a lot of people get the idea that it hardly pays to be honest. This lenient attitude in effect ratifies the system that today dominates much of American life—the system that has enthroned racket czars through a rule of terror on one hand and, on the other, through the lavish use of money for bribery and the purchase of political influence.

One individual case, discovered by the New York commission in the wide-open city of Buffalo, graphically illustrates how such corruption can gnaw at the vitals of organized society. The raids of October, 1959, were only one step in the Buffalo investigations. Much preliminary work preceded the raids, and a special investigation of the Buffalo Police Department followed. In hearings in June and July, 1960, the New York commission spread its findings upon the record.

Carl A. Vergari, an assistant counsel, opening the testimony at these hearings, reported that the commission had been responsible for raiding thirteen bookmaking and thirteen policy operations in Buffalo. In the raids, $52,784 in gambling cash and detailed records had been seized. The records showed, Vergari said, that Buffalo bookies were feeding on a "handle" of more than $100 million a year and that policy was, at the minimum, a $6.5 million racket.

Prostitution as well as gambling was a flourishng trade in Buffalo.

"There were houses of prostitution," Vergari said,

"houses in the classic sense, operated by madams, and in certain cases the entrance to these houses were brightly lit. We have observed as many as ten taxicabs parked outside, with men moving in and out . . ."

The Buffalo Police Department, exhibiting the curious astigmatism that afflicts the law in the presence of big-money rackets, had devoted an exhausting number of man-hours to the difficult task of discovering precisely nothing. Edward L. Morville, an agent-accountant for the commission, analyzed department records and showed that, in twenty-six months, the local precincts had made 14,080 reports. These reports contained notice of the following decidedly minimal discoveries: eight gambling houses, five bookies, no policy operators, no gambling devices, one liquor-law violation, and one vice case. In two years, the Buffalo gambling squad reported 16,730 checkups; it reported "no activity" in 16,446 instances. Here was Buffalo, with a police force of 1,348 uniformed men, 212 detectives, a police budget of $8.5 million a year—here was Buffalo, with the fourteenth largest police department in the nation, although fifteenth in total population, wide open to every kind of racket.

As mentioned earlier, the New York commission discovered that a desk lieutenant in headquarters was doubling as a bookmaker. In private hearings, the commission confronted the lieutenant with betting slips made out in his own handwriting; the lieutenant resigned from the force and claimed the privilege of "the Fourteenth Amendment" [sic] in refusing to answer all questions, even one dealing with the number of years he had served the public as a policeman.

Almost equally significant was the performance on the witness stand of Police Captain William J. Shanahan, who had been in charge of Buffalo's Fourth Precinct for two and a half years. The Fourth was crawling with every kind of law violation known to the evil genius of man, but Captain Shanahan testified that he kept no file on hoodlums, gamblers and racketeers; he didn't know of any gamblers operating in his command, any prostitutes, any houses of prostitution. Had he ever reported any premises as being tainted with even a slight suspicion of gambling? No. Any of bookmaking? No. Any of prostitution? No. Any of liquor-law violations? No.

This sequence irritated Goodman A. Sarachan, the chairman of the New York commission. He pointed out to Captain Shanahan that Mamie Harris had been a famous madam in Buffalo ever since 1922; Sarachan had heard about her then when he first came to Buffalo as a young Assistant U.S. Attorney. "The whole town knew," he said.

"I don't know that, sir," Captain Shanahan replied.

"You never heard of that?" demanded Commissioner Sarachan.

"I read it in the paper here last week, but I don't know of it," Captain Shanahan insisted.

All this forms the background for the most startling testimony of the whole New York investigation. Captain Shanahan was followed to the stand by the most forthright and outspoken witness to appear, Barbara Louise Hartzog, twenty-two, married and the mother of four children. She had lived in the William Street area of Buffalo's Fourth Precinct all her life, and in her unchallenged and uncontroverted testimony, she brilliantly summed up the atmosphere of crime and corruption in Buffalo.

Mrs. Hartzog explained that she had never known a time when the numbers racket did not flourish in the Fourth Precinct. The numbers operators there were so strong, so ruthless, and so greedy that even the normal extortion of their trade wasn't enough for them; they had to have more. In "straight" policy play, the bettor tries to pick a winning three-number combination, anything from 000 to 999. The winning combination is usually determined by a source supposedly beyond and above chicanery —for instance, the last three figures of the U.S. Treasury balance for the day, or the last three figures in the day's pari-mutuel play at a given race track. Though the odds against the bettor's winning are 1,000 to 1, the policy operator normally pays out at only 600 to 1, a disparity that assures him of a highly comfortable margin of profit. In Buffalo, even this margin wasn't enough to appease the insatiable appetite of the racketeers. They shaved the payoff down to 500 to 1 and, in some special instances, to 300 or 350 to 1. Still, thousands played every day on the longshot chance that the skies would open and shower fortune on their heads.

The New York commission asked Barbara Hartzog to explain this addiction in the face of hopeless odds. "Well," she said, "I guess everybody plays the numbers because no one actually, in that neighborhood, had enough money to meet up to the qualifications of living standards in Buffalo."

She explained that she herself played 65 to 70 cents a day on the numbers, even at times when her husband wasn't working. She even played the "night number," an added starter introduced in Buffalo by ingenious racketeers intent on seeing that no hour of the twenty-four was without its potential profit. Since at night there are no new pari-mutuel numbers or Treasury balance numbers coming up, the winning "night number" was determined by three rolls of the dice in a small back room of the Fred

Perry Restaurant at 375 William Street. About a dozen persons would crowd into the tiny cubicle to witness the ceremony. Sometimes Fred Perry would roll the dice; sometimes one of the onlookers would be asked to make the roll—Barbara herself had been chosen for this chore on occasion, she said. A pair of red dice would be rolled to determine the first number of the winning combination; a pair of white dice, the second; a pair of blue dice, the third. While the dice were being rolled, a crowd would back up on the street outside the restaurant, waiting for the verdict.

Q. Would the first roll count or could they change their minds in that place?

A. If they changed their minds, they would change the dice.

Q. In other words, the dice would be rolled and somebody would say, "Well, I don't like that particular number. I want the dice rolled again." Is that correct?

A. That's right.

Q. Was that done on occasions when you were there?

A. That's right.

Q. After the numbers were rolled, was that number announced or posted in any way?

A. It was written on a slip of paper and put up on a paper rack—and hung up, hung up on the showcase.

Q. Out in public view, where everybody could see it, is that correct?

A. Yes.

The questioning then switched to the prevalence of prostitution in Captain Shanahan's Fourth Precinct. Barbara Hartzog was asked whether the extent to which the world's oldest profession flourished there had any effect on a decent married woman. Well, she replied, it was sometimes difficult to walk along the street at night without being accosted. A woman living in the Fourth got used to putting wolves in their place, she said; but late one night, while she was walking home from her sister-in-law's house, she did have a novel experience.

A police car drew up to the curb alongside her, and "This officer stopped the car and told me to come over. I walked over to the car, and he asked who let me out.

"I told him, 'Let me out of where?'

"He said, 'Let you out of the car!'

"I said, 'What car? I just came from my sister-in-law's home,' which I did.

" 'Well,' he said, 'Well, get in.'

"So I got into the police car and they drove around the corner. He says, 'Well, who let you out of the car?'

"I said, 'Out of what car?'

"He said, 'Come off it. You know what I mean.' He said, 'Where's the money?'

"I said, 'I don't have any money. I just—I just left my sister-in-law's house and I got angry with my husband and he left.'

"He asked me for my identification, and I showed him my identification and everything, and he said, 'All right, get home and stay there.'

"It was about 11:30 in the evening."

The incident speaks graphically of the depths to which the Buffalo Police Department had fallen. The cruising policemen had mistaken Mrs. Hartzog for a streetwalker and had been intent upon shaking her down.

The questioning of Mrs. Hartzog switched back to the numbers racket. She explained that this flourished on such a lush, well-established basis that whole books of numbers, known as "B & R books," were issued to regular players.

These were the same kind of numbers books given to runners to sell; but, in Buffalo, the operators had cut another corner by issuing books directly to their regular bettors, making them in effect their own numbers runners.

Mrs. Hartzog had had such a book; she had played a number from it; and then the unbelievable had happened to her—she had beaten those 1,000 to 1 odds. She had won. And then she hadn't gotten paid.

In Mrs. Hartzog's explanation of the persistent efforts she made to collect the less than $100 that was coming to her, the whole picture of the Buffalo policy racket and the open collaboration of police came out. A major figure in the policy ring operated by Fred Perry was Marshall Miles, who had been Joe Louis' manager for a time. He was also, as it happened, a cousin of Barbara Hartzog's own mother. When Mrs. Hartzog began to have trouble collecting on her winning bet, she protested to all the partners in the ring—Perry, Miles, Bonny Kelly, and Pete Craig. "I still didn't get anywhere," she said.

Q. Where did you talk to these men, Mrs. Hartzog?

A. First I talked to Fred Perry in his restaurant, 375 William, and I asked him to pay me because I had turned in the white slip and I had hit the numbers. So he refused to pay me. So I talked to Marshall Miles. He said he would pay me if he had to pay me out of his own pocket.

Q. Did he ever pay you, Mrs. Hartzog?

A. No, he didn't.

Mrs. Hartzog testified that she made the rounds of the policy bosses again. She talked to Perry and threatened to complain to the police if she didn't get her money. He told her he couldn't find her winning slip; it apparently had been lost if it ever had existed, and he wasn't going to pay her without it. From Perry, Mrs. Hartzog went on to Marshall Miles and told him that she was either going to get her money or she was going to the police.

Q. What did he say?

A. He said he didn't give a damn where I went.

So Mrs. Hartzog walked down to Captain Shanahan's Fourth Precinct and went up to the officer on desk duty. Mrs. Hartzog lodged her complaint. She showed the desk officer, she said, the "B & R book" from which she had made her winning play, with the tissue and the yellow second slip for the winning number still in it. "He told me did I know I could get arrested for it," Mrs. Hartzog testified. She replied that, yes, she knew this, but she was determined to collect the money due her and, if she couldn't get it in any other way, she would carry her complaint downtown to Police Headquarters. " 'Well,' he said, 'I can lock you up for just having the slip,' and he said, 'I was going to give you a break and let you go.' "

Mrs. Hartzog left the precinct and started to walk along the street. She explained that Fred Perry, in addition to his restaurant, had an office in the rear of a hat store that she had to pass on her way. As she approached the store, she saw a police car stopped in front of it; and just as she was passing the store, the door opened, and Fred Perry and the desk officer to whom she had just talked at the Fourth Precinct came out. The officer pointed to her in significant sign language that seemed to say, "That's the woman."

Undeterred, Mrs. Hartzog went on to Police Headquarters.

Q. Whom did you speak to down there?

A. Inspector Hahn.

Q. Did you tell Inspector Hahn your story?

A. Yes.

Q. Did he refer you to someone else?

A. Yes, Lt. Ries (Lt. Charles W. Ries, head of the Headquarters Gambling Squad).

Mrs. Hartzog testified that she told both the inspector and the gambling squad commander the full story, naming all the policy operators, including Marshall Miles.

"So they asked me," she testified, "did I want to get a warrant for Mr. Perry's arrest, to see what could be done about it in court. I told him, 'Yes. I didn't want to cause him any trouble. If I get my money, I would just forget it.' So he said, Inspector Hahn told me that, to go back, if I wanted to go back, before they give me the warrant and talk to Fred Perry again and maybe I could get my money. He said to—he says, 'Tell Fred Perry that I said I don't like welshers.' "

Armed with this virtual ultimatum from headquarters, Mrs. Hartzog sought out Fred Perry in the rear of the hat shop. Even this advice from on high had no effect on Perry. "All he said," Mrs. Hartzog testified, " 'I'm not going to pay you for nothing.' He said, 'I can't find the white slip, and I'm not going to pay you.' " She walked out, and he slammed the door after her—hard.

The next morning, much to her surprise, a police car drove up and stopped in front of her home. Gambling Squad detectives got out and told her they had a warrant to raid Fred Perry's Restaurant; she should come with them and identify the woman employee there with whom she had placed her policy bet. "I told them there wasn't going to be anything there," Mrs. Hartzog testified. "Naturally, they knew everything was going to be clean."

She explained that, normally at 10:15 to 10:30 in the morning, the restaurant would be crawling with numbers runners and buzzing with all kinds of betting. But as she had suspected, "the word" had gone out, and the place when she entered it with the Gambling Squad detectives was like a mausoleum. Naturally, the woman who had taken Barbara's bet was not on the premises. Detectives stopped Fred Perry, who was just going out the side door as they came in, and questioned him. He was asked if he employed the woman Mrs. Hartzog had named as the bet-taker. Never heard of her, Fred Perry said. Well, did he know Mrs. Hartzog? The policy boss looked hard at Barbara. Very hard. Never saw her in his life, he said.

Naturally, it was obvious to the law that no arrests could be made, no action taken. The detectives gave Fred Perry and his restaurant a clean bill of health. It was a certificate of good conduct that they renewed after another so-called "inspection" on October 22, 1959—just twenty-four hours before state raiders crashed the policy bank and exposed both the rackets and the police of Buffalo.

4

CRIME'S PERFECT GOVERNMENT

THE most powerful crime syndicate in the nation, historically, has been that of New York City, and so it should come as no surprise that, when 150 delegates to a high council of crime met in Worcester, Mass., in December, 1959, their ties to the top hierarchy in New York appeared to be especially close. After all, it was from New York that Johnny Torrio and Al Capone went west to organize the mobs of Chicago; it was the New York Syndicate that dispatched Buggsy Siegel to California to develop the rackets there, and when Buggsy got so independent he had to be removed from the scene, it was the New York mob that designated a successor to look out for syndicate interests in the Mecca of legal gambling he had pioneered in Las Vegas. These and many other operations involving millions—gambling in Las Vegas, in Louisiana, in Florida and in Havana, Cuba—have demonstrated time and again the long reach and the fundamental importance of the New York mob in the councils and activities of the underworld.

It is almost elemental, then, that to understand what is taking place in the underworld today one must understand the composition of the modern New York Syndicate, and this can only be understood if one understands the past from which it has sprung. For the New York mob today is the heir of one of the most fantastic criminal organizations America has ever known. This was the Frank Costello-Joe Adonis combine, dominant in American crime for nearly twenty years; and anyone who would get a clear picture of the unholy alliance of crime and politics must appreciate the example of this classic crime cartel.

Costello and Adonis were headline names during the Kefauver investigation of 1951. They were denounced as the rulers of the Eastern Syndicate, and a vast amount of detail about their ties and influence was spread upon the public record. But neither then nor since was the full story ever presented, nor did the public ever get any idea of the government of crime they perfected and ran for nearly a decade with perfect immunity from the law.

It was an immunity so strong that it actually turned the forces of the law into a protective shield for gangsters. It was an immunity that found local police in Bergen County, N.J., watching with tender solicitude over the homes of Joe Adonis and Albert Anastasia—and chasing out of town any detectives who came spying on these overlords of the underworld. Even investigators from the office of District Attorney Hogan in New York, even U.S. Treasury agents got what can only be described as the bum's rush.

When local police shoo even Treasury agents out of town, the final and complete perversion of the law has been accomplished. The man who masterminded this achievement was Joe Adonis, born in Italy as Joseph Doto, known to the mob as Joe A. In the days of his power he was stockily built (5 feet 7½ and 190 pounds) with hard brown eyes and dark brown hair turning gray. He dressed with the expensive conservatism of a millionaire; he affected genteel manners; he kept his voice always soft and low-pitched; in outward appearances he was a perfect gentleman.

Joe Adonis, who had been brought to America by his parents when he was a child, had grown up on the tough South Brooklyn waterfront, and he had never had any ambition except to become a gangster. Possessed of one of the shrewdest minds in the rackets, he rose fast. He was an intimate of Charles (Lucky) Luciano, the Mafia chief who became the first over-all czar of the New York rackets, and his relations were equally close with Luciano's successor, Frank Costello. The major reason for these tight ties was simple: Joe Adonis commanded the enforcers—that infamous band of killers known as Murder Inc.

Albert Anastasia, notorious throughout the underworld as the Lord High Executioner, was in direct charge of the assassination squad employed by syndicates all over the nation to enforce their edicts; but above Anastasia was Joe Adonis. For years Joe A. was the "Mr. Untouchable" of Brooklyn. He financed political campaigns, and at one time he had at least a third of the Democratic leaders of the borough in his hip pocket. His tavern was the rendezvous for the Borough Hall crowd—the meeting place for local politicians, state legislators, prosecutors, and judges. Even when William O'Dwyer broke up the Murder Inc. ring in 1940 and sent some of its most eminent members to the electric chair, he did not touch the two men who really mattered—Anastasia and Adonis.

Joe A., who had achieved eminence without ever making the acquaintance of a prison cell, then transferred the base of his operations. Brooklyn, with the Murder Inc.

probe going on, was inhospitable, and so Joe A. sought out a more salubrious atmosphere. He found it just across the Hudson River, in Bergen County, New Jersey, hard by the western end of the George Washington Bridge. Here, within view of the spires of Manhattan and just outside the jurisdiction of New York law, Joe A. set up a veritable capital of crime—the nerve center for the rackets in the East.

His throne room was in the rear of a dingy tavern known as Duke's, located at 783 Palisades Avenue, Cliffside, New Jersey, directly across the street from Palisades Amusement Park. Here Joe A. presided over a Council of Five, soon to be known in the underworld as the Big Five, and here he sat day after day, running the affairs of crime.

It would be ludicrous, if it were not tragic, to contemplate the innocence of the American public about the mechanics of big-league crime. The convocation of sixty Mafia leaders at Apalachin, N.Y., in November, 1957, made headlines throughout the nation. Reading them, one got the impression that no such thing had ever happened quite this way before; the general public retained the impression that Apalachin was unique, supremely important, and especially dastardly. Actually, it was almost routine. For the plain fact is that nothing as gigantic as big-time crime can operate without a board of directors and without staff conferences. No multi-billion dollar business can flourish without planning, executive decisions, and the enforcement of its directives. What is true of legitimate business is even more true of the illegitimate, which, in addition to the complications inherent in the handling of billions, faces intricate problems in the arrangement of clandestine deals, the guarantee of protection, the establishment of elaborate protective fronts.

Of the Crime Council that sat in Duke's—the Big Five—the undisputed ruler was Joe A. himself. At his right hand sat the man who always had followed his fortunes—Albert (Big Al) Anastasia, the master of murder. Next in their order of importance came two local contact men—loud, brash, wisecracking Willie Moretti, and his smaller, darker, more quiet shadow, his brother Salavatore (Solly) Moretti. And last but by no means least came the man who to this day has generally managed to avoid the public spotlight, Anthony (Tony Benda or Tony Bender) Strollo, long known to the Federal Bureau of Narcotics as the chief lieutenant of Mafia chieftain Vito Genovese.

The existence and the rule of this council were documented in the investigations of unimpeachable agencies, especially by the office of District Attorney Hogan in New York and the Federal Bureau of Narcotics. Hogan's men, in particular, uncovered details of Adonis' technique. When a job was to be performed, Joe A. would send out his summonses to small, medium, and major mobsters all over the city of New York. Jumping into their Cadillacs and Chryslers, they would scuttle across the George Washington Bridge and gather about the bar at Duke's, there to wait, sometimes for hours, for the call from the inner throne room that would assign to each his special mission. Sometimes Joe A. would summon three times the number of mobsters he could possibly use, just to be certain that, if some unforeseen contingency should arise, he would have the man he needed.

Not just the daily work of crime, but larger sessions devoted to grand strategy were held inside Duke's. According to the Federal Bureau of Narcotics, Tuesday was meeting day for what might best be described as the legislature of crime. Regularly each week some twenty criminal overlords and their henchmen would gather in Duke's to confer with Joe A. and the Big Five. The delegates would arrive between noon and 1 P.M. "The big men drive their cars into a large garage which is two doors north on the same side of Palisades Avenue," the narcotics bureau noted in one confidential memo. "The rest park in the general vicinity."

To such gatherings came some of the biggest names in the American underworld of the day. Frank Costello, known to big-time gangdom as The Boss or the Prime Minister, would come from New York in his chauffeur-driven Cadillac. Abner (Longy) Zwillman, the old Newark bootleg czar who had become a major power in New Jersey politics and one of the biggest men in the Eastern rackets, would arrive from his home in West Orange. Meyer Lansky, the original partner of Buggsy Siegel in the infamous "Bug & Meyer" mob and still today a reigning power in the colossal gambling activities of the underworld, might drop in from Saratoga or Miami. These and many others, men like Gerardo (Jerry) Catena, who has now advanced to a dominant position in the Jersey rackets, huddled regularly with Joe A. to map Syndicate strategy.

This system worked smoothly for years, and no investigative agency in New Jersey raised so much as an inquisitive eyebrow. As the Kefauver Committee was to show in its later, partial look into the Jersey rackets, one prominent local police chief hobnobbed with the mob right in Duke's, and in case after case, representatives of the law developed a truly astounding affluence, keeping thousands of dollars in safe deposit boxes or bank accounts. There were two favorite explanations of this wealth: inheritance from a rich relative fortuitously deceased, or an especially remunerative private business. In some ten

Bergen County towns clustered along the Palisades, agents of the law repeatedly demonstrated either that they were most fortunate in their relatives or the most perspicacious of businessmen.

Meanwhile Joe Adonis and his Council of Five turned the entire North Jersey area into the richest Syndicate satrapy east of the Mississippi. This was the mob's own estimate of the value of its gambling preserve, as given subsequently to investigators for District Attorney Hogan. Indisputably, in Bergen County, every kind of gambling racket ran wild.

The county's location was strategic. It was just a convenient short hop away from New York City across the George Washington Bridge, and so became the haven of New York mobsters and the repository of the great city's gambling wealth. In New York itself, until the mid-1940's, the late Fiorello LaGuardia ran a Fusion administration devoted to banishing the influence of the New York underworld. It was an eternally frustrating battle because the mob had found that handy refuge just across the Hudson. Time and again LaGuardia shouted shrilly on the radio: "We've chased the tin-horns [his contemptuous phrase for gambling moguls] out of New York, but they've fled over the bridge to Jersey." No law-enforcement authority in New Jersey paid any heed to these public complaints.

Joe A. had so many wide-open rackets running that it makes a man's head swim just to contemplate them. First came the bookies. There were three prongs to their operation. The first involved horse-race wire-rooms that literally honeycombed Passaic County and parts of neighboring Bergen. A chartered limousine service picked up horse players at selected spots in midtown, downtown, and east-side Manhattan. The chauffeur-driven cars rolled in a steady stream across the bridge, drivers waving casually to friendly cops as they deposited their clientele openly at horse rooms on the main streets of Paterson and other North Jersey cities. These rooms were elaborately equipped. They were cluttered with chairs and tables at which the addicts might sit and contemplate their scratch sheets; they had regular betting booths and raised platforms manned by men with earphones who received the results directly from the tracks and posted them on a board. There was no possibility of secrecy about horse-rooms flourishing on such a scale, with literally thousands of New Yorkers being transported daily to their rendezvous with chance; but the system ran for a long time, unhindered by New Jersey law.

The second branch of the bookmaking conspiracy was conducted on an even more grandiose scale. This consisted of a telephone network set up especially to handle heavy play from New York. In the city itself, LaGuardia had made it hazardous for bookies to conduct their business in their normal manner; and so, with the co-operation of certain elements of the Police Department that not even LaGuardia could purify, the Syndicate established an intricate and artful system. Runners collected bets and deposited them at selected drops. Then, from pay phones, the compiled play was sent across the Hudson to New Jersey, where, in Bergen County, a far-flung network had been set up to receive it. The size of this network was in itself convincing evidence of the colossal amount of play, for to handle bets from the great metropolis, the Syndicate had to rent 2,600 phones. The system worked like this: an agent for the mob would offer a householder $50 a week for the privilege of using his phone for a few hours each afternoon. The $50 weekly fee was a windfall for the average citizen, who did not have to work to earn it and who usually was not even inconvenienced. Daily an agent of the mob would show up at his home, establish himself at the telephone, and for a few hours conduct a fast and furious business. Usually, by suppertime, the agent had departed as quietly and inobtrusively as he had come. If New York snoopers later checked the phones—as they did—all they would find was that the enormous flow of betting from New York was being channeled into the homes of reputable citizens. There was no tie to identify the agents of the mob.

The corruptive effects of such a system were almost infinite. One official estimate later pegged at *$4 billion a year* the amount wagered over this network, with gross profits reaching into the hundreds of millions. No illicit operation, obviously, could run for years on such a scale without cast-iron protection; but in Bergen County the influence of mob money extended far beyond the normal bounds of officialdom. In Bergen large segments of the general public, too, became corrupted. The householder who was receiving that $50 a week in quick and easy money became convinced that there could be nothing wrong with a little gambling.

Topping both of these operations was a third—the "layoff" business of Frank Erickson, the so-called king of the bookies. Erickson established his "layoff" center in Bergen, and there, as he later testified, he provided insurance for bookmakers throughout the nation. The "layoff" bets flowed into Erickson's headquarters from every state, and Erickson himself, in what seems like a modest estimate, admitted that he did a $12.5 million annual business. Even after dispensing his loot with a lavish hand (for example, he paid one man $20,000 a year just to bank his money for him), Erickson reaped an annual reward many of the highest paid business executives in the nation might have envied. Even in his worst years, according to his own federal income tax returns, he never made less than $100,-000, and in 1946 he reported a net of $194,841. When a bookie czar in a prosperous year receives almost double the pay of the President of the United States, it should become fairly obvious that, while we cling to the pretenses of a moral society, we do not live by our professed standards.

The extent of bookmaking in Bergen County gives some idea of the enormous power of the rackets, but this was not all. For to this torrent of gambling cash that flowed into Bergen County Joe Adonis added another golden stream—a veritable cascade reaped from suckers who patronized his elaborate gambling casinos.

Bergen County, even before the advent of Joe A., had been historically no stranger to big-time casino gambling. In fact, throughout the Thirties, one of the most famous gambling houses in America had operated brazenly from the very cliff edge of Hudson Terrace, just north of the New Jersey end of the George Washington Bridge. This was a nightclub known as Ben Marden's Riviera, and the fantastic play that took place in its Marine Room became the talk of the nation. For years, the Riviera was a brilliantly flaunted scandal, and time and again, in Bergen County, reformers vainly attacked it and the corruption it represented. Though the reformers made no headway, the wide-open Riviera operation was an invitation to trouble; after Joe A. transferred his headquarters to Bergen in 1941, he swiftly changed the system. Joe A. was too wily an operator to flaunt his illegality; he shunned the publicity that serves only to arouse opposition. And so the Riviera was sold and became what it remains today, a legitimate nightclub; Joe A. devoted his talents to developing a string of equally remunerative, but far less conspicuous casinos, spread out over the countryside.

His technique was to seek out the most drab, inconspicuous structures he could find—an abandoned factory, an old barn, a Quonset hut. Retaining their shanty-like exteriors as a camouflage, Joe A. then would lavish a fortune on interior renovations designed to create an atmosphere of elegance and glamor. From $75,000 to $150,000 would be spent in face-liftings: costly furniture, ankle-deep rugs, original paintings. The cuisine would be exemplary, the service flawless. Waitresses and cigarette girls were chosen for their striking beauty; croupiers and stick men in the gambling rooms wore full dress. Everything was swank.

Such were Joe A.'s so-called "carpet joints." One of the most famous of these was established in 1945 in West Paterson in Passaic County, just over the Bergen County line. The site at 1025 McBride Avenue had been purchased for $22,500 in cash, a small fortune had been spent on interior renovations, and a staff of fifty employees kept dining hall and gambling rooms functioning in style. The Federal Bureau of Narcotics, keeping a close watch on all Joe A.'s operations, discovered that the profits of this one house were equally stylish. In December, 1945, Narcotics Agent Ross B. Ellis estimated that "the average nightly 'play' over three crap tables, four roulette wheels, and three chemin-de-fer tables is considerably in excess of one million dollars." The bureau felt that it was being most conservative in estimating that the gross profit to Joe A. and the Morettis must amount to at least *$100,000 a week.*

At the same time that Joe A. was reaping a nightly fortune in his West Paterson "carpet joint," he was piling up equally impressive amounts of cash from a "sawdust" crap game in South Plainfield in Middlesex County. A "sawdust" game is just what the name implies—a comparatively crude gambling establishment, with no swank decorations, no elaborate kitchen, just a simple sandwich bar. The "sawdust" game in South Plainfield was located in a concrete-block, garage-like structure down a lonely road, and a taxi fleet from New York and Newark, shuttling steadily back and forth through the night, regularly brought a stream of several hundred players to its tables. Ross Ellis, scouting the premises in December, 1945, found two guards armed with sub-machine guns patrolling the road. Ellis reported that there was only a single table at which pikers could gamble for as little as $5 a throw. Other tables had $10, $20, and $50 minima, and on one the play was for $1,000. Ellis concluded that "several hundred thousand dollars pass over these tables each night."

Such a tremendous concentration of underworld gambling activity can hardly exist for years undetected by the law. Taxi fleets and chauffeured Cadillacs can hardly run day and night without attracting attention. Horse rooms can hardly operate only a few feet off the main streets of well-patrolled cities without the cops knowing. In New Jersey, repeated public exposures reinforced common sense.

LaGuardia and his successors in New York took an almost impish delight in needling New Jersey authorities. John Murtagh, when he was Mayor William O'Dwyer's Commissioner of Investigations, issued lists of Bergen County telephone numbers used by bookies to handle play from New York. Newspapers frequently exposed the Jersey rackets. The Newark *Evening News* focused a strong spotlight on the West Paterson game and recognized it as a Joe Adonis enterprise; the Hudson *Dispatch,* in one issue, devoted most of page one to a prominent, large-type display of the telephone numbers being used by the Bergen bookies. On the floor of the New Jersey State Senate, one Democratic legislator charged that the underworld was reaping a gross profit of *one million dollars a day* out of the Jersey rackets and challenged the Republican administration to order an investigation. The Republicans squelched the demand. Despite this embarrassing public furor, nothing happened seriously to inconvenience the mob.

When newspaper exposés caught up with his gambling games, Joe Adonis simply closed them down and moved on to new locations. His organization was so efficient it could dismantle a "carpet" joint and move out all its plush furnishings and equipment at an hour's notice. Members of the mob bragged quite openly that they always knew when "an inspection," as they called a raid, was about to be held, and events seemed to indicate this was no idle boast. Repeatedly representatives of the law crashed the doors of Joe A.'s "carpet" and "sawdust" joints. Always they arrived just too late; always, they found the premises swept bare of all incriminating evidence.

Such fiascos of course had repercussions, but the repercussions were smothered quickly. The authorities always rode out the temporary tempests, and the general public, with only a vague and partial knowledge of the magnitude of the evil, didn't seem to care. Together Joe A. and the Big Five flourished in Duke's, and a Republican "reform" administration flourished in Trenton.

To understand this supreme irony, one has to have at least a sketchy picture of Jersey politics. Throughout the Thirties, the political life of the state had been dominated by one all-powerful boss—Mayor Frank Hague, of Jersey City. The Hague Democratic machine in populous Hudson

County made a practice of voting even the names on tombstones, and by this and other devious practices, frequently produced such an avalanche of votes that heavy Republican margins in rural sections were smothered. The Republicans, if they were ever to dethrone Hague and make their own rule supreme, needed a populous, one-sided county to counter-balance Hudson. They found the answer to their need in Bergen, and the Bergen County Republican machine, well-financed and powerful, began to run up such heavy majorities that Hudson and Hague could no longer control the state.

A major beneficiary of this development in the late Forties was New Jersey's Governor, Alfred E. Driscoll. Driscoll had come into politics as a reformer, an opponent of machines and boss control; he had made a record as an independent in the State Senate, and he had been an able Alcoholic Beverage Commissioner. But his nomination and election had been made possible in 1946 only by the whole-hearted support of the Bergen County organization, and his campaign manager had been John J. Dickerson, the man generally recognized as the boss of the Bergen machine. As Governor, Driscoll performed with an efficiency that has been rarely matched in New Jersey. He achieved the drafting of a new state constitution, the consolidation of sprawling government departments, the revamping of the state's archaic judicial system. Such accomplishments led many to compare him to Woodrow Wilson and to rank him with the greatest New Jersey Governors. In his whole performance there was just one flaw; throughout the three years of his first administration and well into his second, both Driscoll and his Attorneys General maintained a hands-off attitude regarding the repeated charges of corruption in Bergen.

Joe Adonis and the boys in Duke's continued to revel

in the fabulous financial returns of their racket empire. They might have been reveling yet except for a wild mischance. On a Wednesday night, July 28, 1948, a so-called "charity gambling party" was held in the swank penthouse apartment of Mrs. Vivienne Woolley-Hart on New York's Park Avenue. Lurid accounts of the party filled the gossip columns of the New York press and caught the eye of District Attorney Hogan. He ordered an investigation.

Hogan's chief assistant was then Vincent A. G. O'Connor. O'Connor, aided by Assistant District Attorneys Andrew J. Seidler and James J. Fitzpatrick, wasn't long in discovering that, though Mrs. Woolley-Hart had had no suspicion of the truth, the gambling conducted in her apartment had been an extremely professional operation, bearing no resemblance to the innocent games of a church bazaar. Hogan's aides learned that the charity that had been supposed to benefit had withdrawn its sponsorship of the affair at the last minute; and by questioning those who had gambled and lost, investigators soon learned the vital details of the evening's action. Nineteen dealers had manned tables devoted to roulette, chemin de fer, bird cages and dice, and some of those who had played and lost told Hogan's men they had seen some of those nineteen faces before—across the Hudson, in New Jersey's gambling halls.

Fortunately for Hogan, unfortunately for the mob, many of the guests at the Park Avenue party had gambled away all their cash and had had to write out checks to cover their losses. It is often hard to determine what becomes of cash, but checks leave a distinct trail. And when Hogan's investigators followed this trail, they found an unsuspected quarry.

The checks all had cleared with a New Jersey check

casher named Max Stark. When detectives began prying into Stark's activities, they encountered a financial operation so colossal it challenged human credulity. Max Stark, whose real name was Mendel, was a short, obese man who draped three chins above his collar. He lived in Teaneck, in the heart of Bergen County, but fortunately for Hogan's men, he had preferred to transact much of his banking business in New York. He held a 10 per cent interest in the Merchants Bank of New York, and to this bank, on every working day of the week, he came lugging satchels crammed to bursting with bills of all denominations. By questioning bank officials, Hogan's investigators learned that it was a slow day indeed when Max Stark hefted as little as $30,000 through the bank's portals. Often he would bring in $50,000 and sometimes as much as $90,000. The bills were always crinkled and stained with the sweat of the previous night's losing agony in the Jersey halls of chance, and the entire sum had to be counted and recounted so that these bedraggled bills could be exchanged for the crisp, new greenbacks with which the gambler likes to tempt his customers.

When Hogan's aides resorted to a little addition, they struck a total for this daily cash traffic of Max Stark's that made their eyes pop. Stark, their calculations showed, had been hauling at least $200,000 a week into the Merchants Bank of New York. He had done this week after week, with no letup, and when Hogan's aides multiplied $200,000 by 52 weeks in the year, they gazed down in astonishment at a figure that pyramided to more than $10 million. Yet this figure, startling as it was, was far from the whole story. For Max Stark, in addition to cash, handled checks.

An examination of his accounts in the Merchants Bank of New York showed that in 25 months from 1946 to

1948 he had deposited $6,810,847 worth of checks. When detectives questioned persons whose checks had cleared through the account, they learned that all, without exception, had been heavy losers in the Jersey gambling casinos. Max Stark was the human conduit for a tremendous flow of gambling millions, and when Hogan's staff added the millions in checks to the millions in cash, they struck a grandiose total. They established that, at a minimum, the annual play in the North Jersey gambling halls came to $13.5 million. "Actually, that figure was ultraconservative," O'Connor explains. "We felt certain that this was probably closer to a $15 million to $20 million-a-year operation."

Any enterprise so mammoth had to be a major project of the Syndicate; Hogan's investigators, by questioning the signers of checks that had passed through Max Stark's accounts, quickly got the full story. The losers, in their tales of misfortune, pinpointed the location of the major Adonis gambling enterprise of the moment.

In 1946, Joe A. had established a new casino in a Quonset hut in back of a gas station on Route 6 in Lodi, New Jersey. The hut became known as Costa's Barn. It began as one of Joe A.'s most splendid "carpet" joints. The dining room was presided over by a maître d'hôtel who was later to establish his own famous New York restaurant; food and drinks were on the house; all that was required of the sated guest was that he compensate by playing and losing his money.

Hogan's investigation showed that Costa's had gone through two phases. In its early days, all a wealthy New Yorker had to do was to dial a Passaic number, give his name and address, and specify the time he wanted to leave. At the appointed hour, a Cadillac with liveried chauffeur would draw up in front of his apartment or hotel, ready to whirl him across the bridge to the game. In May, 1948, Joe A. demoted Costa's to a "sawdust" joint. The individual chauffeur service was abandoned, and players had to catch a ride from a midtown parking lot where two dispatchers worked throughout the night keeping a fleet of twenty Cadillacs rolling back and forth to the game. Even under this more subdued and more economical operation, some 250 to 400 players were transported nightly to the barn in Lodi.

Not only the system but the men who ran it were identified in the evidence compiled by Hogan's aides. All agreed that Joe A. was on the premises almost every night; and though he didn't actually run any of the tables himself, he was clearly the supervisor of every phase of the operation—"the boss, the lord of the manor," as O'Connor puts it. Aiding him was another of the shadowy directors of crime at Duke's—Willie Moretti's quiet and efficient brother, Solly.

Word of the District Attorney's activities filtered back to the mob in Jersey. Adonis reacted swiftly. On August 17, 1948, he closed down the Lodi game. The following day Frank Erickson suspended his "layoff" operations, and the 2,600-telephone bookie circuit went dead. Throughout the underworld rumbled the dire phrase, "The heat's on."

New Jersey officialdom, so long silent and unheeding, broke out in a rash of reaction. One North Jersey Prosecutor rushed over to beat on Hogan's door and departed wreathed in smiles of relief when he was told the mess wasn't in his county. He had hardly left when Driscoll's Attorney General, Walter D. Van Riper, arrived. O'Connor and Seidler in a long conference spelled out the full details of what they had learned to Van Riper; they described for him the exact location of Costa's Barn, identified Joe Adonis as the mastermind of the enterprise, and supplied the names of several of the dealers and credit men. Hogan's assistants emphasized to Van Riper the importance of Max Stark as the financial key to the whole conspiracy, and they stressed that what they had learned came from examining just one Stark bank account. Stark had other accounts, in New Jersey banks, and his full business records were there. Seizure of those records would produce far more evidence than Hogan had been able to obtain. Van Riper left, promising a thorough investigation.

Hardly had he disappeared when another delegation arrived upon the scene. This was headed by Michael J. Orecchio, a former plumber whom Prosecutor Walter G. Winne, of Bergen County, had elevated to the post of chief of county detectives. Winne was a power in the Bergen County Republican machine headed by Dickerson. In conducting the affairs of his office, as much later testimony was to show, he relied more heavily on Orecchio than on his own legal assistants, and so it was not unusual that, on this particular day, the former plumber should have been delegated to be the eyes and ears of the Prosecutor. Once more O'Connor and Seidler spelled out the full details of the operation in Costa's Barn. They even had their detective chief draw a road map showing Orecchio exactly how to get there, and the Bergen detective chief left, breathing promises of action.

And then nothing happened.

Within two days Prosecutor Winne was protesting that all Hogan had given him was "rumors." He said he had doubts whether there even was such a place as Costa's Barn. Van Riper performed a little better. He did at least pick up Max Stark's records. The records were turned over to Winne. And Winne reported that he had accountants examine them and had found that the checks clearing through Max Stark's accounts were those of reputable businessmen, not racketeers! This, of course, was true, and, as O'Connor and Seidler had so patiently explained, it was the very reason that the records were so valuable. The "reputable businessmen" were the gamblers' victims and potentially, as Hogan had already demonstrated, invaluable witnesses against them. But Prosecutor Winne called no witnesses. The seized records were given back to Stark, and New Jersey took no action against him.

This collapse of New Jersey law left everything up to Hogan. With a wealth of evidence in his hands, the New York District Attorney was nevertheless severely handicapped, for he had no jurisdiction in New Jersey. Trying to find a way around this dilemma, Hogan initiated a conspiracy action against Max Stark, contending that Stark had conspired in New York to commit a crime in another state. At the same time, hoping to catch the Bergen County mobsters crossing the river and committing some overt act in his own jurisdiction, Hogan dispatched his detectives to set up watch over the homes of Joe Adonis and Albert Anastasia.

The instant he did, he encountered trouble. New York detectives hardly had a chance to park their car down the street from Joe A.'s mansion before local police came cruising along. At first, expecting or at least hoping for co-operation, the New York detectives identified themselves. They quickly found that their status as officers of the law gave them no status with local cops. "Come on, move on," the local officers told them. "It doesn't make any difference who you are. Nobody is allowed to park around here."

U.S. Treasury agents encountered the same persistent obstructionism. The narcotics bureau had funneled Ross Ellis' estimate of the huge play in the Bergen gambling dens to the Internal Revenue Bureau, and Treasury men, like Hogan's agents, tried to snoop around in Bergen. But the instant they did, they found local police shadowing and harassing them. "It got so bad," one Treasury investigator said later, "that that SOB —— (naming the police chief in one Bergen town) would be on our tails almost the minute we crossed the bridge."

Behind the buffer of such cast-iron local protection, Joe A. reopened all his temporarily discontinued rackets. The bookie telephone network went back into action; Frank Erickson reopened his "layoff" headquarters; Joe A.'s own big gambling games roared wide open again. Hogan tried to throw a shadow across this mob paradise beyond the Hudson by securing the indictment of Max Stark and one of his assistants for conspiracy. In a trial in New York, both men were convicted, but later, on appeal, won a reversal on the technical ground that Hogan had not proved *the actual deed of conspiring* took place in New York. Despite this setback, the New York District Attorney went ahead with his investigation, trying to build a tighter legal case against Joe Adonis.

For nearly two years after the exposure of 1948, Joe A. and the mob continued to reap their harvest of millions.

No one can say how long they might have flourished in, if to the threat posed by Hogan in New York, there had not been added a second—that posed by Kefauver in Washington. In the summer of 1950, the Senator turned a partial spotlight on the highly odorous North Jersey scandal. He picked up Hogan's revelations about Max Stark's multi-million dollar bank account and exposed lush profits piled up by a number of dummy corporations Joe Adonis had created to take care of the bookkeeping details of some of his gambling enterprises. And finally he summoned to the witness stand several North Jersey policemen and drew from them illuminating testimony about the thousands of dollars in cash they had packed away in safe deposit boxes. Typical was the testimony of Police Chief Frank Borell, of Cliffside Park. Borell, who received a salary of only $4,500 a year but said he made a handsome profit from concessions at Palisades Amusement Park, displayed an amazingly casual attitude about money. Asked how much he had in banks, he replied: "Approximately $50,000, $60,000, $70,000. It could be $80,000 or so." Even such testimony did not arouse any zeal for action among New Jersey officials. Kefauver began to get angry.

The Senator made his feelings clear in conferences with Nelson F. Stamler, the rackets-busting specialist in the New Jersey Attorney General's office. Stamler, a ruggedly built six-footer, had been used by both Attorney General Van Riper and his successor, Theodore D. Parsons, in various cleanup missions throughout southern and central New Jersey. In these activities, he frequently exchanged information with Hogan's office, and as early as January, 1950, Hogan's aides had briefed him in considerable detail on the case they were building against Joe Adonis. Knowing this, Stamler appreciated the seriousness of Kefauver's threat that, if New Jersey did not clean its own house, the Senate committee would expose the full mess in public hearings. Stamler urged Attorney General Parsons to act at once and head off trouble. Parsons, he said, gave every indication that he wanted to act, but he didn't.

Despite Kefauver's pressure, despite Hogan's imminent action, New Jersey officials still stalled. Finally, Kefauver, losing patience, told Stamler bluntly that his committee intended to subpoena Governor Driscoll and compel him to testify. This, it seems, was the final straw. On October 20, 1950, Stamler was named to supersede Prosecutor Winne in Bergen County and to conduct a probe of gambling and official corruption. The action came a full two years and two months after the Woolley-Hart disclosures, two years and two months after Hogan's office had spelled out explicitly for New Jersey officials the racket operation in Bergen and Joe Adonis' role in it.

Once Stamler was given authority, results were quickly achieved. With the help of Hogan's office, Stamler swore out warrants on October 30, 1950, for the arrest of Joe Adonis, Solly Moretti, and three of their lesser henchmen. The following day, the mobsters walked into the Bergen County Courthouse and surrendered. Pressure on the gambling moguls was now swiftly intensified. Just nine days later, on November 9, a New York grand jury returned a criminal information accusing them of conspiracy to violate New Jersey's gambling laws. This double threat brought a swift and surprising reaction from the mob.

On a Sunday night, November 12, 1950, a gangland delegation descended without warning on the home of State Republican Chairman John J. Dickerson, the powerful Bergen County boss who had been for so long the campaign strategist of Governor Driscoll. The only full version of what was said at this meeting was the one Dickerson gave two years later to a New Jersey Legislative Committee. The Republican leader said he had been loafing in pajamas and bathrobe around his home in Palisades Park when the doorbell rang and he went to answer it. Confronting him on the doorstep was stocky, balding Willie Moretti. Behind Willie loomed the figures of Solly

Moretti and Joe Adonis. Dickerson led the delegation down to his basement playroom, and there Willie Moretti acted as spokesman.

"He said he was tired of being pushed around up there in Bergen County; that he had paid out a lot of money and that he didn't intend to take this laying down, and I believe he used a term 'unless something is done about it, he is going to blow the lid off' and language along that type . . . ," Dickerson testified.

"So I said to him, 'Well, what do you come to me about this situation for?'

"And he said: 'Well, you are . . . state boss, you are state top man of the Republican Party and we want this stopped.' "

Dickerson said that he had protested he knew nothing about any arrangements Willie Moretti had made and demanded to know whom Willie had been paying. Willie then charged that he had paid $12,000 a month for 19 months, a total of $228,000, to Harold John Adonis (no relation to gangdom's Joe Adonis) who had been a publicity man in Governor Driscoll's campaigns and had served as a clerk in the Governor's office in Trenton. According to Dickerson, Moretti told him: "Of this $12,000, $10,000 was going to Governor Driscoll and $2,000 was being given to Harold Adonis for handling it."

Dickerson said the whole story left him shocked and incredulous. He testified he told Moretti "no one can ever sell me on the idea that the Governor ever got a dime" and "I think you have just been sold down the river." Willie Moretti, however, refused to be put off. He insisted that Dickerson take up the matter with Attorney General Parsons and said he would return the next night for an answer.

What happened next makes a long and confusing

story. The State Legislative Committee spent months delving into it without ever achieving final and satisfactory answers, and only the main outlines can be sketched here. The morning after the visit of the three mobsters to his home, Dickerson told Attorney General Parsons the full story, then drove to Trenton and talked with the Governor. Driscoll, who always exhibited great pride in his administration, was furious. Moretti's whole yarn was a bare-faced lie, he said. Dickerson was told the Bergen investigation certainly would not be halted; it would be pressed to a finish. When Willie Moretti came back that night for his answer, Dickerson told him neither the Attorney General nor the Governor knew anything about the bribe he said he had paid and that the probe would proceed. Willie, Dickerson said, turned on his heel and walked away without a word.

Now began, as the legislative committee later found, a curiously laggard investigation into the sensational Moretti bribe charges. Harold Adonis, who had been discharged from his duties in the Governor's office more than a year before, was allowed to leave the country and go to South America. He later returned, motored leisurely through several states with his wife and family, and left once more for South America. The state had evidence that he had been spending large sums of cash, but at no time was any close watch kept on his movements, nor was he approached or questioned. For approximately two more years, Willie Moretti's account of the $228,000 gangland bribe remained a skeleton in the political closet, its very existence unknown to the public, the state investigation of it virtually a dead letter.

In the meantime, the fate that the mob had tried to forestall befell it. Joe Adonis, Solly Moretti, and their three lesser associates were indicted for operating Costa's Barn. The mobsters tried to drive as soft a bargain as possible with the law. Their agent in the negotiations was their attorney, John E. Selser, a former assistant to Winne in the Prosecutor's office. Selser testified that he had many conferences with Attorney General Parsons; that Stamler, who was the special prosecutor in charge of the Bergen probe, was kept in the dark about all of these; that an agreement was finally reached for treatment so considerate that the mob was, if not pleased, at least satisfied. Relying on the agreement, the mobsters pleaded *non vult* (no defense) to the gambling charges against them. They anticipated sentences of 18 months to two years, fines that they could well afford to pay—and no probation. That last provision was especially important, for a racketeer on probation courts danger every time he associates with his equals. He can be slapped right back into prison for hob-nobbing with shady characters like himself; and if he is to avoid this penalty, he must pay, and pay heavily, for the law to blink at his acts. At all costs, Joe A. and his cohorts wanted to avoid this danger.

For this reason, they were content with the arrangement Selser had negotiated with Parsons, and pranced into court on May 28, 1951, jaunty and smiling. The brief court proceedings, however, changed all this. Smiles turned to scowls. For the treatment the gangsters got was not the treatment they had expected.

The jail term was lengthened to from two to three years, the fines were increased and, worst of all, each mobster was doomed to five solid years of probation after leaving prison. This was disaster. Willie Moretti, who had a great fraternal affection for Solly, was visibly outraged. Outside the courtroom, in the corridors of the Bergen

County Courthouse, he screamed to Stamler: "You can't do that to my brother!"

Willie Moretti had lived by the code of gangdom all his life, and a cardinal tenet of that code is that the mob must always protect its political protectors. If face has to be saved, if certain sacrifices have to be made to the law, this must be accepted as one of the inevitable hazards of the business. But under no circumstances must "the fix" be jeopardized. Otherwise it will be just that much more difficult for the surviving Syndicate, once the fuss and furor has died down, to make new arrangements and to continue doing business. Perhaps one of the most graphic examples of this philosophy in action was furnished by the Murder Inc. probe in Brooklyn. Abe Reles, the killer who turned State's evidence and sent fellow assassins to the electric chair, bragged repeatedly of the underworld's extensive influence in high circles, but he always balked at supplying details. Not even Reles would betray the system of bribery and purchased influence without which the Syndicate cannot live. Neither, it would seem, would Willie Moretti under any circumstances except those which existed now. But much evidence seems to indicate that Willie, outraged at the treatment his brother Solly had received, was being driven toward the ultimate indiscretion—that he was about, as he had warned Dickerson, to "blow the lid off."

Stamler talked to the disgruntled Willie that spring of 1951 before Willie departed to spend the summer at the New Jersey shore. Willie gave Stamler the impression that he was almost, but not quite, willing to talk. He was tempted, but he still had considerable faith in his influence, and still felt that he could work out a deal to soften Solly's punishment. Stamler was convinced that Willie couldn't, and so he let Willie go, trusting to time and frustration to do their work.

On September 27, 1951, as Stamler later testified, he and Willie met in the corridors of the Bergen County Courthouse. Willie was flipping his lid. He told Stamler that he had always operated "just like the president of a racetrack, strictly pari-mutuel"—his way of saying the politicians had always taken their cut—and that he was ready to go before the grand jury and "testify against plenty of people."

"What people?" Stamler asked.

"Some of the county leaders," Willie replied.

Stamler declared that he whipped out a subpoena and served it on Willie on the spot. Stamler was content to wait until October 10, when the grand jury was to meet again, to get the all-important details of the Bergen fixes from the one man who knew them and could tell all.

What happened next was something that Stamler hadn't anticipated.

On the morning of October 4, 1951, just six days before he was scheduled to appear before the Bergen County grand jury, Willie Moretti drove to Cliffside Park. Duke's, where the Council of Crime had sat for so long, had closed its doors, and Willie and his cronies had fallen into the habit of meeting in Joe's Elbow Room at 793 Palisades Avenue, just down the street. On this particular morning, Willie's chauffeur parked Willie's shiny, new, cream-colored Packard convertible near the Elbow Room a few minutes before 11:30 A.M. Willie got out, leaving a well-marked racing sheet he had been studying on the seat behind him. As he started toward the door of the restaurant, a man who had come out on the sidewalk apparently looking for him rushed up, shook hands effusively, and followed him into the Elbow Room.

There three other men were gathered around a table waiting for Willie. They all stood up when he entered. They all shook hands and jabbered away in a tongue that the waitress, Mrs. Dorothy Novack, felt certain was Italian. The atmosphere was like that of old home week when Mrs. Novack left the restaurant to get some silverware from the kitchen.

Hardly had she disappeared when the most infernal racket broke out. Fearfully, the startled waitress and the kitchen help peered through the door. The four men who had been waiting for Willie Moretti had vanished. Only Willie remained in the restaurant, and he lay sprawled out on the floor, blood spreading in a pool around his bullet-shattered head.

This murder blew the lid off the long-suppressed Jersey scandals. In the aftermath of Willie Moretti's murder, Stamler became involved in bitter feuds with his superiors, Attorney General Parsons and Governor Driscoll. The rackets-buster felt that the investigation of the Moretti murder should have been placed in his hands; but it wasn't. Stamler was disgruntled. He felt—and the state investigation later showed that he was absolutely correct—that the investigation was being bungled. Weeks passed before detectives even got around to taking one of the elemental first steps in such an investigation—canvassing the area for potential eyewitnesses; the prosecutor in charge subsequently admitted that he never read the State Police reports; and nobody on any level showed any disposition to make a possible connection between the long-suppressed story of the $228,000 gangland bribe and the murder of the man who had said he paid it.

The Bergen County grand jury under Stamler's direction began to delve into the almost neglected $228,000 bribe story. On November 7, 1952 it returned the first of two indictments against Harold Adonis and Willie Moretti, charging conspiracy to obstruct justice. This action exploded the long-hidden scandal into the ghastly prominence of page-one headlines, and there is considerable evidence that high officialdom in New Jersey was definitely displeased with Stamler. In the wake of the indictment, Driscoll, Parsons, and Dickerson all praised each other for the roles they had played, but significantly, nobody praised Stamler, the man who had achieved the result of which, ostensibly, everybody was so proud.

Tension continued to mount. Soon Stamler was criticizing his superiors, not just for bungling the Moretti murder case, but for botching up the Harold Adonis case as well. His personal relationship with Parsons became intolerable, and finally in January, 1953, the Attorney General went to Hackensack and summarily fired his rebellious deputy. The action precipitated a new storm. Bergen County grand juries that had worked closely with Stamler came to his defense and made it clear they felt he had been hamstrung in attempting to get to the bottom of the corruption in Bergen. And Stamler has maintained ever since his belief that "gunmen hired by politicians murdered" Willie Moretti.

Such, in essence, is the story of the rise and long-continued sway of a mob government, financed by gambling rackets, that practically dominated a county and spread tentacles of influence throughout an entire state. The later performance of the law showed little improvement. A few gamblers went to jail, but that was all. Stamler's grand juries had indicted local police, municipal officials, even county officeholders. Almost without exception nothing happened to any of them. In some cases local juries acquitted the defendants; in others, convictions were thrown out on appeal. In time many of the cases lapsed. Only one man received really severe punishment. Harold John Adonis, the one-time $4,100-a-year Governor's clerk who had built himself a fancy home from mysterious cash resources, paying out $43,892 in one twelve-month period, served a five-year sentence in federal prison on an income-tax evasion charge. After his release, he was tried in Bergen County on the conspiracy-bribery indictment—and acquitted. Former Governor Driscoll, who had gone from politics into business, hailed the verdict as proof that Willie Moretti had been nothing but a liar.

Moretti's murder remains unsolved.

This is the kind of boxscore that is typical of almost every crusade against the mob. Not even the horrified national reaction caused by the Kefauver exposé could force a cleanup down to the grass roots. What happened in Jersey is what usually happens: a few heads roll, the law is pacified, the headlines die, and the system goes on.

The Crime Council that sat for so long in Duke's, it is true, underwent partial dissolution—but its heirs are still among us. Joe Adonis, imprisoned for his Bergen County gambling activities, later was faced with a federal deportation action and departed for voluntary exile in Italy. Willie Moretti was murdered. His brother, Solly, died in New Jersey State Prison in Trenton. Albert Anastasia, the Lord High Executioner of the old Murder Inc. was deactivated for a time by a federal income tax indictment, served a short prison term, and when he emerged, discovered that the new order was passing him by. When he refused to yield his power and prerogatives, he was gunned out of a barber's chair in a midtown New York hotel in the broad daylight of a late October morning in 1957—a public execution that, like almost every other deed of its kind, remains unsolved. By this process of elimination, today only one of the Big Five remains.

Anthony (Tony Bender) Strollo, the least conspicuous member of the old crime board, was left with all the threads of Syndicate organization in his hands when the exposés of 1951 terminated the careers of his fellow councillors. A real estate man and the owner of Greenwich Village nightclubs, Strollo has been described by District Attorney Hogan as a dominant underworld power on the lower Manhattan and Hudson County waterfront and by FBI experts as heir to the power of Frank Costello. For more than twenty years, the Federal Bureau of Narcotics has listed Strollo as the chief lieutenant of Mafia chieftain Vito Genovese, and it is indisputable today that the New York criminal axis pivots about the Strollo-Genovese combine. The henchmen who have come to power, men like Mike Miranda and Vincent (Vinnie Bruno) Mauro, are closely linked to Strollo; and Carmine Galente, one of the most powerful and dreaded underworld figures in the East, was tied to the same power group when he was named as a defendant with Genovese in a narcotics case.

These are the new powers in the East, heirs of the old. Except for Genovese, who made the mistake of getting himself convicted on the federal narcotics charge, they have largely escaped the glare of headlines. But investigators on many levels are aware of their presence and their power; no one who has any conception of the tremendous gold mine represented by the New York gambling rackets, as demonstrated so vividly in Bergen County, suffers from the delusion that the New York mob has turned its back on such a reservoir of fabulous millions. It has changed and refined but still bankrolls an empire of crime by a profit of millions reaped annually from the gambling rackets of the nation's richest metropolis.

5

THE NEW YORK RACKETS

ONE of the greatest mysteries in American crime in the last ten years revolves around the simple question: What happened to the New York City bookmaking racket? After the Kefauver investigation, the city's multi-billion dollar bookmaking industry, a traffic so huge that a 2,600-telephone circuit in Bergen County had been required to handle it, suddenly went underground. It disappeared from view like a witch on a jet-propelled broomstick.

Time and again occasional probes have spotlighted huge bookmaking operations in lesser cities, but New York itself has remained one vast and intriguing blank. Elsewhere large-scale bookmaking leaves clues through the manner in which it gets "the line" from Minneapolis or arranges "the layoff" in Covington. But in New York City, traditionally the largest "action" spot in the nation, these conventional ties fade out—they cease to exist.

One might almost come to the conclusion, if one were naive enough, that bookmaking has withered and died inside the city. High New York City police authorities occasionally encourage this belief. Oh, yes, they say, there is some betting, it will always go on, you can't eliminate it entirely—but there is nothing big, nothing overt, no syndicate operation. The facts refute these pretensions. Anyone who has worked or lived in New York, and kept his eyes open, knows that it is just as easy to get a bet down on a horse or a football game as it ever was. It is not unusual for several small bookies, each with his own clientele, to split up the trade in a single large office building. The man on the street knows that this traffic goes on just as it always did, and the incongruity between what plainly exists and what probers have been unable to find provides one of the most tantalizing mysteries of the day. A clue to that mystery was provided for the first time during the New York State Commission of Investigation probe.

The commission's objective was upstate gambling; it had not proposed to inquire into the separate problem of New York City. Yet it would be only natural to expect that many ties to the great New York City underworld would have appeared. After all, upstate bookies were in constant touch with Minneapolis, Covington, Biloxi, Detroit, Chicago, Boston and Miami. But—and this was the truly amazing circumstance—not with New York City.

"Oh, there was a telephone call or two, but nothing significant, nothing at all like what you would expect," Bill Walsh explains. "For all practical purposes, ties between the city and upstate simply did not exist."

Joseph Manners, of Milton Wessel's federal rackets-busting team, had been perplexed in his earlier investigation by the same vacuum. He had pieced together telephone contacts across the nation and had established interlocking relationships between massive bookmaking operations in many states. But he had found these links vanish when he came to New York. After much intensive study, Manners came to the conclusion, as Walsh did after him, that the

New York City bookmaking racket was the most skillfully directed and the most sophisticated in the entire nation, and that it operated behind the façade of some highly respectable fronts.

"I always leave New York City out," Manners said in his testimony before the New York commission. "It's a confusing area. It just didn't seem to tie in all the way around. So many hotels being called frequently, and different room numbers up there."

Later Manners again put his finger on the hotels as the key to the New York riddle. He explained that his investigators, like the state sleuths, had been unable to establish any significant ties between city and upstate books. "We could not work the New York City area because of . . . all the many hotels involved," Manners declared flatly. "We could not get the proper information."

What emerges is that the bookmaking racket has taken refuge behind a front of respectability that many of New York's fine hotels provide. The hotels may know what is going on, but as long as they don't object the bookmakers operating from their shelter enjoy almost ideal protection from the law. One major advantage to the books, for instance, is the virtual impossibility of tracing and identifying their telephone calls. How does one sort out the calls funneling into hotels containing hundreds of rooms? How does one determine which calls are legitimate calls, and which bookie calls? Even wiretapping becomes impossible, for though tapping is legal in New York with a court order, the order must be based upon evidence that a particular phone is being used for an illegal purpose by an individual. Courts frown, for example, on the tapping of pay telephones, which are used by the general public as well as the bookies, on the theory that the police have no right to listen in on the conversations of a number of law-abiding citizens in their hunt for one illegal user. Obviously, the same rule applies to the flood of calls passing through a hotel switchboard.

The books of New York shun such crude techniques as the individually registered phone and the private business that is a transparent cover for illicit operations. Rather, they seek anonymity in the large number of legitimate customers patronizing apparently respectable places. It is perhaps not entirely by chance that heavy mob investments have been poured in recent years into the nightclub and hotel businesses. One member of the bookmaking fraternity insists that the largest book in the nation makes his headquarters permanently in one of New York's most famous East Side nightclubs. Another Mr. Big of the bookmaking industry is described as a man who, in the late 1940's, before Kefauver, was sometimes handling a play of $500,000 a day. He now runs a women's dress business as a sideline, makes his bookie headquarters in a respectable East Side hotel, and presumably does a business that has grown in the past decade with the growth of gambling nationally.

Knowledge of the covert New York City bookmaking industry does not depend only upon such grapevine reports, however reliable. Certain concrete items crept into the New York commission's record as by-products of the upstate probe. Though the city's gambling fraternity had managed to avoid most of the interstate ties that betray their racket to federal probers, though they had shunned tell-tale links to "the Minneapolis line" and "the layoff" in Covington, there was one essential service without which even the New York books could not exist. This was the receipt of fast results from the track. And fast results meant reliance on the Tollin service in Wilmington, Delaware.

The Delaware Attorney General's office had obtained a list of all the code names representing Tollin customers, and Detective Wassmer, during the New York inquiry, began to go through the list, identifying the upstate towns in which the Tollins had bookie clients. Most towns were represented by a single name, perhaps two; even large cities had relatively brief listings. But when Walsh, who was questioning Detective Wassmer about what the Tollin list disclosed, came to Manhattan, he turned up *six solid pages of code names.* Since the city had been left outside the scope of the state inquiry, Walsh was flipping past the pages without comment when Commissioner Grumet interrupted and called attention to this proof of the extent of Manhattan's bookie trade.

"There are six pages of subscribers right here in Manhattan," Grumet pointed out.

When Walsh totaled the number of names on the Tollin list, he found that results were being flashed daily from Wilmington to 150 books in New York's five boroughs. These were almost certainly just the major operators in the city. As the New York commission had found in its upstate probe, Tollin results are relayed by major books to lesser figures in the trade; in fact, some books made a business out of pirating Tollin results and charging their own string of smaller books for the relay of the information. The significance of the discovery that the Tollins service 150 books in New York City lies, then, not in the number itself, but in what that number represents. The entire Tollin list showed that this was the heaviest single concentration of customers anywhere in the nation, or, as Walsh phrased it, New York City books were "the best customers the Tollins had."

A subsequent discovery by the New York commission

confirmed the size of the New York City racket and gave for the first time an indication of the manner in which it is linked to national syndicates. In the final compilation of evidence amassed in raids and wiretaps, Bill Walsh and his investigators became curious about the tie that had been exposed in the one telephone call made by Joe Vizzi to Al Mones in Miami. How important, they wondered, was Mones? Just how extensive were his dealings in New York State? A check with federal investigators revealed that, during one very brief period, federal agents had compiled a telephone analysis showing all the calls that went out from Miami over Al Mones' line. This analysis established that Mones had been in constant contact with bookies throughout the nation. He had carried on a steady telephone traffic with 405 bookie numbers in New York State. Of these 205 were in New York City.

"We would never have picked up this pattern on our wiretaps," Walsh explains, "for Mones had one hard-and-fast rule—nobody called him, he always called them. That one time Joe Vizzi broke the rule and phoned him was the only call we could be sure of in our investigation. Of course Mones may have called Vizzi while we were tapping Vizzi's wire, but if so we had no way of knowing who he was or where the incoming call originated."

This total of telephone numbers called does not necessarily mean that there were exactly that number of books in touch with Al Mones, Walsh carefully explains. In order to reduce the risk of detection, books often switch telephone numbers, and so one book may be transacting business over two or three different numbers. However, as Walsh also points out, the federal telephone analysis covered a relatively brief period of time, and this means that there couldn't have been too much switching, that those 205 numbers Al Mones called in New York City are still a pretty fair indication of the magnitude of the bookmaking operation there.

Such a major operation, cloaked in such secrecy, means inevitably that the underworld in New York City has perfected a racket organization of the highest order. Such an organization can operate only through the tightest mob control—the allocation of territories, the dictation of business details from the top, the rule of kangaroo courts and enforcers. This system has revealed itself in many wiretaps made by the office of District Attorney Edward S. Silver in Brooklyn. The District Attorney testified before the New York commission that bookies had been overheard asking each other questions like: "Who is the Combination from South Brooklyn that is doing all that betting?" and, "What group are you working with, out of whose territory are you working?" The New York racket is so systematized, Silver said, that it is impossible for a lone bookie to set up shop. The District Attorney testified that anyone who "thought he could pick himself out a corner some place in New York City and begin making book, would receive a rude shock to find that he could not do it without an okay from the boys who are taking care of the situation."

So huge and powerful is the New York City operation that it extends its tentacles far beyond the boundaries of the city itself. Charles R. Thom, Suffolk County Police Commissioner, described how the rule of the New York mob has been extended clear to the eastern tip of Long Island, some 120 miles from downtown Manhattan. Until about two years ago, Thom said, bookmaking in Suffolk County had been a local operation run by the corner butcher or the neighborhood barber; but then the New York Syndicate, composed of Manhattan and North Jersey gambling moguls, began to move in. Its weapon, he said, was money in fabulous amounts; muscle and murder were shunned because "the mob is still afraid of local juries."

"Money is the ammunition of the Syndicate," the Suffolk commissioner declared. "Pressure is on bettors as well as bookies, especially if the bettor is a business proprietor. Bettors get wined and dined and the average $10 bet rapidly expands to a $100 bet or greater. And, once hooked, the bettor faces financial disaster. Even otherwise respectable housewives have been led into unfortunate practices."

These "unfortunate practices," Thom explained later, involved what he called "afternoon prostitution." In a few cases, he said, gambling housewives had become so indebted to bookies that they were forced into this extra-marital activity in an effort to balance their accounts.

The tremendous bankroll of the New York mob literally bought it control of the Suffolk bookmaking racket, Thom said. He enumerated three major advantages of the new syndicate system which Suffolk bookmakers had found irresistible.

1. "Unlimited resources with absolute backing which eliminated the need to 'lay off.'" In other words, Suffolk bookies no longer had to worry about balancing their books to insure their "vigorish"; they no longer had to hunt a "layoff" center to take care of their dangerous play. All was being handled for them by the New York Syndicate.

2. "New York City telephone numbers could be passed along to regular bettors and players, which made the bookie merely a collector of money, credited on the books of the Syndicate through an efficient bookkeeping system, and adding the tremendous factor that use of the telephones was thus changed, greatly reducing the efficacy of telephone taps." In other words, a Suffolk bookie no longer needed

to run the risks inherent in individual phone use; the play of his clients could be funneled directly to the cop-proof, wiretap-proof phones the Syndicate had established behind respectable fronts in New York.

3. In case something went wrong, "the Syndicate agreed to provide 'stand-up men' where feasible"—in other words, bums who could be hired for perhaps as little as $50 to take gambling arrests as stand-ins for actual bookies.

The extension of this system from Manhattan through Brooklyn and Queens and Nassau Counties and out into Suffolk is in itself a vivid demonstration of the power of the New York Syndicate. This power, this enormous concentration of gangland wealth, helps to explain the manner in which the New York mob, except for the Tollin service, has managed to operate as a separate entity, flourishing with few tell-tale contacts with the rest of the nation.

New York investigators are still not certain about the manner in which the city books get "the line" from Minneapolis. One possible explanation is that here, too, they operate behind apparently legitimate fronts. Hirshfield brags, after all, that he supplies his services to sports writers, and it would seem entirely feasible, considering New York's many publications, to get the changes in "the Minneapolis line" through agencies that have no apparent tie to bookmaking.

The solution to the other mystery, why the New York City books do not "lay off" in either Covington or Biloxi, is even more simple and more startling. They do not "lay off" simply because their operation is so huge that they do not have to.

It must be remembered that even the big play, the dangerous play, is in the long-run losing play. It is only because books cannot take the risk of being "hit" by a single heavy winner that they seek insurance in the "layoff," and "layoff" centers in turn seek further protection through investing "comeback money" at the tracks. But if a gambling syndicate has a bankroll so heavily padded with millions that a heavy winner, even a series of heavy winners, cannot seriously dent it, then there is no necessity for seeking an outside "layoff"; this operation, whose major function is to insure the "vigorish," can be financed internally because the inevitable long-run percentages are always against a bettor's winning. All the evidence indicates that the New York mob is the happy possessor of such a bankroll.

The point was hinted at in the New York hearings, not only in the testimony of Commissioner Thom, but in that of New York's First Deputy Police Commissioner, James R. Kennedy. James Kennedy, who for years had been the gambling-racket expert of the New York Police Department under Commissioner Stephen Kennedy, was asked:

"In the case of bookmaking, has it been your finding that New York bookies, however large and however important they may be in bookmaking, confined their operations almost exclusively within New York City?"

"I would say yes," Kennedy answered.

Commissioner Grumet asked for an explanaion of this, and Walsh said:

"I think, perhaps, Commissioner, it may be attributed to the fact that the capital available to the gamblers in New York is sufficiently great. They have been able to act as their own 'layoff' group."

Privately, Walsh expresses the opinion that there must be occasions when the New York Syndicate finds it advisable to deal with Covington or with Montreal. "For example," he says, "if the New York Yankees are playing the

Chicago White Sox at Yankee Stadium, it stands to reason that the betting in New York is apt to be far heavier than in Chicago. If the local books become overloaded in such a situation, it would seem to me that they would have to do business with the Chicago books, and arrangements for a 'layoff' would have to be made." The discovery of Al Mones' telephone contacts in New York would seem to indicate that, when such a necessity arises, the "layoff" play could be relayed to Miami and distributed from there —a system that obviates the giveaway of New York books making out-going calls directly to "layoff" centers.

The colossal size of the gambling racket in New York has been underlined by official estimates put out by the administration of Mayor Robert F. Wagner. The Wagner administation has, in effect, pleaded guilty to being unable to curb bookmaking and has advocated its legalization. The administration annually tries to persuade the State Legislature in Albany to permit it to legalize off-track betting in the city as a revenue-producing measure. Mayor Wagner's experts estimated that a 15 per cent tax would return $200 million in revenue to the city and state, a figure that was considered ultraconservative. Actually, Robert W. Dowling, who headed the Mayor's Citizen's Committee for Off-Track Betting, predicted that the tax would bring in much more and estimated that illegal bookmaking in New York "now reaches $5 billion a year."

Such seemingly fantastic figures do not seem quite so fantastic when one recalls that a 2,600-phone bookie network in Bergen County *did* exist and that the best possible estimate of its play, based in part upon seized records, placed it at $4 billion annually. That was more than ten years ago, and all the evidence indicates that gambling has grown into an even larger business in the interim. Even officials who have no desire to magnify the racket are forced at times to concede at least the possibility of its size. Police Commissioner Stephen Kennedy, in his testimony before the New York Commission of Investigation, pointed out that legalized betting at New York tracks in 1959 fell just shy of $1 billion. He noted that, in countries where off-track betting has been legalized, the off-track play averages from two to five times the on-track betting, and he acknowledged that, if such percentages held true here, New York City has a "huge" problem. Since bookies themselves place the ratio at four or five to one and consider a three to one ratio far too low, it seems highly probable that the illicit bookmaking industry in New York City is fattening on a fantastic $3 billion to $5 billion annual flow of bets.

But even this is not all. To the take from bookmaking must be added the take from a rival racket, one hidden in no such obscurity but operating in the broad light of day —policy.

Betting on the numbers was considered a major underworld gold mine back in depression days when Dutch Schultz's policy empire flourished in Harlem and the Bronx and lured a gross annual play, in nickels and dimes, of $20 million a year. Nickels and dimes hardly rate as money any more; now the play is for fifty cents or one dollar, even for ten dollars or more, and now the racket isn't confined to the slums of Harlem and the Bronx. It runs rampant there, of course, just as it always did, but to the daily tribute of the poor, there has now been added that of the middle classes. Policy today has spread all over the city of New York, even into the skyscrapers of Wall Street, where the principal gambling interest is supposed to be the stock market.

A couple of years ago I walked into a downtown Broadway office building one wintry day and stood listening to the elevator man make his pitch to a woman worker in the building. "Did you get your number today?" he asked. "No," she said, "I haven't got it yet. You know, I'm beginning to think that's a racket. Nobody ever seems to win." The elevator man slowly shook his head in solemn disagreement. "Oh, no," he said, "somebody always wins, somebody's got to win. There are an awful lot of people playing, you know, but every day somebody wins. You better get your number before it's too late." The woman thought it over. "Well, I don't know," she said, "I'll see. Maybe I will."

The spread of the policy racket throughout New York City that this incident symbolizes had been widely confirmed. Early in 1960, reporters from the New York *Journal-American* and the New York *Post* made careful surveys and came to the conclusion that the numbers game was big business in every section of the city. The *Post* staff estimated that the numbers written every day on the waterfronts of Manhattan, Brooklyn and Staten Island exceeded the best day's "action" in Harlem; that the play in Manhattan's garment district was equally huge; and that the big money bet on the numbers in the financial district around Wall Street made the racket larger there than in the Bedford-Stuyvesant section, the Harlem of Brooklyn.

Estimates of the size of the racket vary. The most reliable appears to be the unofficial assessment put together by one wing of the federal investigative team that operated under Milton Wessel. Treasury investigators worked for six months under the direction of Wessel's aide, William Esbitt. They examined the records of several hundred policy cases disposed of in New York's Court of Special Sessions and questioned a large number of policy operators. Essentially, this is what they discovered:

1. The play for one hundred working days in the

policy racket in the city reached a gross of $500 million. This estimate was reached by totaling the play of known policy operators for the test period and averaging this out with the number of policy operators reliably reported to be working in the city. Projected on a full-year basis, this would mean that policy in New York is a $1.5 billion racket.

2. Evidence of high organization and tight control was clear. Questioning of arrested policy operators invariably produced the same story: the lowly hired hands were the agents of a syndicate; they did not know who the bosses were; all they knew was that they worked on a percentage of the play they brought in and were assured that, if arrested, they would be taken care of—that when they appeared in court bondsmen and lawyers would be there to represent them.

3. The key to the racket, the go-betweens who linked the racket bosses with the hired hands who occasionally got arrested, obviously were these same bondsmen and lawyers. Examination of court records covering the disposition of several hundred policy cases showed that a small group of less than a dozen lawyers was handling the major portion of the syndicate's policy business. One attorney in a year handled 445 cases; another, 326; a third, 299. Efforts to question some of these lawyers were futile; interestingly enough, the attorneys claimed, not the privilege of a lawyer-client relationship, but the Fifth Amendment against possible self-incrimination. Balked investigators were convinced that, if these lawyers ever talked, they could provide the details on the organization of a racket that was apparently being masterminded by remote higher-ups in Florida and Las Vegas.

4. Obviously no racket could flourish for years on such

a scale—especially a racket like policy that must operate day in and day out from fixed locations—without widespread corruption and political protection extending high into various echelons of the city government.

The findings of Esbitt's investigative team were reinforced by a series of public disclosures made in New York's Special Sessions Court by the new presiding justice, John M. Murtagh. Murtagh began to mete out jail terms to gamblers and called pointed attention to the bondsmen-lawyer conspiracy. In stiff questioning of policy defendants appearing before him, Justice Murtagh showed that their cases were handled by bondsmen and lawyers hired in advance—men whom the defendants themselves didn't even know. In early March, one 71-year-old defendant, who had been arrested with 294 policy plays in his pocket, was brought before the justice. A $500 bond had been already written out for him.

"What did the bondsman tell you?" Justice Murtagh demanded.

"He told me to come here today."

"Did he tell you anything about a lawyer?"

"He told me to see him when I got here."

"What's your bondsman's name?"

"I don't know his name."

"Did he say that he would have a lawyer for you?"

"Yes."

Under the law it is illegal for a bondsman to solicit a lawyer for a defendant, and a fine of $500 and a year's jail sentence can be imposed for the offense. Yet the cases in Justice Murtagh's court showed that this provision was constantly flouted. It was customary for lawyers to come into court with prepared lists containing the names of defendants whom they had never met. In most cases the lists had been drawn up by bondsmen, who made arrangements for their own fees, the lawyers' fees, and any fines that might be levied, in a package deal with the operating powers of the syndicate. In Justice Murtagh's view, the bondsmen and lawyers whose services had been engaged even before the men they represented had been arrested were as much a part of the conspiracy as the numbers runner on the street—and a far more vital part because their contacts went much higher.

When the underworld is so well organized, corruption is inevitable. The extent of that corruption in New York was illustrated when Justice Murtagh discovered that the policy ring had been able to falsify records forwarded to the court from the Bureau of Criminal Identification in Police Headquarters. This bureau is one of the most heavily guarded units of the department. After a defendant is fingerprinted, his prints are taken to the Bureau of Criminal Identification; there they are compared with those in the file, and a "yellow sheet" containing the full record of the man's criminal career is prepared. The information that is contained in the files of the BCI is vital in many fields of detective work; it is, or it is supposed to be, sacrosanct.

But on April 7, 1960 Robert Beaman, a 36-year-old policy collector in Harlem, having been caught with 281 policy plays in his possession, was brought before Justice Murtagh. He was fined $100. No jail term was meted out because the BCI "yellow sheet" showed that this was his very first arrest. A court stenographer with a long memory recalled, however, that he had seen Beaman's face before and reported his suspicions to Justice Murtagh. An investigation by Murtagh turned up the true BCI record, which showed that the defendant with the supposedly "clean" past had been convicted no less than fifteen times previously on policy charges. In the uproar that followed, it developed that falsification of the most vital records in Police Headquarters was an established practice. The going rate for this record perjury was reported to be from $2,500 to $3,500. The fake "yellow sheets" were on official forms and bore the true imprint of the seal kept in the Bureau of Criminal Identification, indicating that someone in this nerve center of the Police Department was implicated in the racket. All a gambler need to fix up his past when he appeared in court was money. If he had the fee, he could exchange a long and dirty record for a lily-white one—and so avoid the unpleasantness of jail.

These disclosures, added to the detail amassed by Esbitt's federal investigative team, pressured a probe by District Attorney Hogan. A New York County grand jury, under the direction of Hogan aides, spent several months poring over the evidence and listening to 135 witnesses. Finally, on October 18, 1960, the jury acted. It returned a presentment.

In this the jury expressed proper shock and horror—and regretted that unfortunately it was legally impossible to indict anybody. The grand jury investigation did substantiate the key contention of Esbitt's federal group and of Murtagh that there appeared to be a small ring of lawyers and bondsmen who were virtually kept on a retainer basis by the policy syndicate. Naming no names, the jury said it had found evidence that some ten lawyers and six bondsmen had been on the payroll of policy racketeers. This ring handled more than 60 per cent of all the policy cases in Manhattan, and the jury denounced as "unethical, improper and reprehensible" the supplying of such "mass-production protection."

Despite this finding, the jury couldn't see its way clear to indict any of the bondsmen or lawyers. It merely ordered that the secret minutes of its hearings be sent to the Appellate Division of Supreme Court and the State Insurance Department, agencies that have the power to disbar lawyers and to refuse to license bondsmen. Since no racketeer has ever yet been crushed by the harsh words of a presentment—especially a presentment cloaked in such delightful anonymity—the Hogan probe would seem to have produced little more than a fiasco.

A similar investigation of the BCI record-fixing charges produced only a slightly better result. In late September Hogan's office secured the conviction of William Smith, a Brooklyn lawyer, on four counts of conspiracy and conduct unbecoming a lawyer. Testimony showed that Smith had represented three policy defendants whom he knew to have past records, that he had told Justice Murtagh they had no records, and that he had backed up this assertion by exhibiting to the court clean "yellow sheets." Though Smith was convicted, a specific charge that he "switched or caused to be switched" the vital arrest records was dropped, and the whole issue of the record forgery and the manner in which it was engineered was left unresolved.

This less than sensational performance of the law took place in the face of a series of sensational charges made on the floor of Congress throughout the winter of 1960 by Representative Adam Clayton Powell, the preacher-politician from Harlem. Whatever one thinks of the flamboyant Powell, this much must be said for him: he comes from Harlem, he knows it intimately as few men do, and when he begins to name names and give addresses of flourishing policy spots, his information is usually accurate.

Powell charged that the Police Department was permitting policy to flourish as a wide-open racket in Harlem and that, furthermore, under the aegis of virtually official approval, the local Negro policy bankers were being driven to the wall by the Italian mob and a few Jewish helpers. Ironically, New York officialdom seemed more to resent the charge of racial discrimination in permissive rackets than it did the real meat of Powell's allegations—that it was permitting the racket to operate in the first place. There was a great outcry because the Congressman had injected a racial charge into the controversy, but Powell, undeterred, continued to blast away with weekly charges on the floor of Congress.

In a series of speeches he pinpointed specific policy spots in Harlem; he charged that a former member of the Bureau of Internal Revenue had quit his federal post to become "the numbers boss of lower Harlem"; he named as "bagman" an officer attached to the staff of the Police Academy, who, he said, called regularly each month at policy spots in Harlem to collect "the pad"; finally he read into the record an itemized list of payoffs exacted each month by police from numbers spots.

"Each numbers banker has to pay from $2,500 to $3,500 a month in protection ranging from the top of the division down to the lieutenants, sergeants, uniformed officers, two shifts of radio cars, all the detective squad including plainclothesmen, lieutenants and sergeants," Powell charged. He submitted a detailed breakdown of the payoff, based on a complaint that had been filed with the New York Commission of Investigation. The complaint read:

> To operate with protection all policy spots are required to have a contract with the various offices

of the Police Department. Such a contract is generally referred to as a "pad." All pads are due on the first of the month, and must be paid not later than the 3rd.

The list below is a breadown of a policy pad. The totals that are followed by an asterisk (*) vary in proportion to the number of men assigned to the precinct. The total cost of the pad may reach as high as $3,000 a month, due to fluctuations in the number of men that are carried by a given office.

Division	$420
Borough Headquarters	$275
Police Commissioner	$275
1st Deputy Commissioner	$275
Chief Inspector	$275
Precinct	
Captain	$50
23 Sergeants at $10	$230*
8 Lieutenants	$160*
Uniformed officers on post	$192*
Radio Cars (2 shifts)	$192
Detective Squad	
33 Detectives	$330*
Detective Lieutenant	$ 50
Detective Sergeant	$ 25
Total	$2,749

Officers on post and officers in radio cars are paid daily, all others are paid, in advance, monthly.

The payments listed in this memorandum are obviously group payments. The fact that an entire detective squad is paid does not mean that every man on the squad is a crook; some presumably cannot be bought. Similarly, the payments listed to the Police Commissioner's office and the First Deputy Commissioner do not mean that either Stephen Kennedy or his deputy, James Kennedy, are personally involved; both are considered in New York to be high-class police executives, and the Commissioner has frequently been mentioned as a possible successor to FBI Director Hoover. What the memorandum does purport to show is that the total payoff is calculated on the basis of the maximum number of offices and individuals that have to be taken care of for total protection. This is how the bite is figured; this is the money paid. Who gets it, precisely, is another question.

Powell went on to outline the real significance of New York's flourishing syndicate gambling. He pointed out in explicit terms that the question was not simply one of betting, but of the narcotics peddling and violence and murder that are the evil partners of betting. He said:

"When I began this crusade there were people saying, 'Why argue against the numbers? Everybody gambles.' That may be true, but we do not want gambling to be the backbone of narcotics. I do not believe there is any man who is in favor of that except the gangsters themselves. . . .

"I should like to point out that one combination of thugs has just been revealed to me. It is a combination called Sam and Mannie. It operates drugs and numbers together. . . . When a James Russell came to my church two Sundays ago, he was scared to death because these two men, Sam and Mannie, thought he was conveying information to me. He was not. I never heard of him. He came to me and begged me to protect him. The result is that this past Friday night James Russell was badly beaten and is in serious shape. In 1956 a man who worked with them by the name of Charles Turner was also beaten by Mannie and Sam, and later his body was found floating in the East River in the Harlem area."

The New York *Post,* in its own investigation of the policy racket, confirmed the most startling of Powell's charges—that concerning the size of the "pad." The *Post's* information came from both policy operators and sources inside the Police Department itself. The newspaper quoted one police official as saying frankly: "If you knew the actual amount of money involved, you wouldn't believe it. And even if you believed it, the *Post* wouldn't print it. The thing is just that big."

To get some idea of just how big the "thing" is, the *Post* figured out the "ice," or protection money, that was being paid by policy in just one section of Harlem. Its survey showed that there were ninety approved policy spots running in this single section. Each was paying off, at a minimum, at a rate of $2,500 a month. Multiply the monthly figure by the number of spots, and you get more than $220,000; multiply by twelve months in the year (not even bothering to figure the traditional "double ice" at Christmas time), and you get a pay-off of more than $2.5 million. And this for just ninety policy spots in just a single section of Harlem!

Policy, remember, now flourishes in every district of the vast, sprawling city of New York. The *Post,* quoting a police informant again, put it this way: "There are eighty precincts in New York City, and in my experience in all five boroughs, I have not found a single one in which a 'pad' for policy isn't maintained in one form or another." The total "pad" will not be as heavy in many districts, of course, as it is in policy-ridden Harlem. Nevertheless, it is obvious that a $2.5 million annual pay-off in just one section of Harlem must represent only a tiny fraction of the over-all corruption; that the total take, from policy alone, must build up into a truly staggering sum of money.

But this incredible vista of corruption represents only half of the total picture. For policy is, if anything, the lesser of New York's two great gambling rackets. Bookmaking, all experts agree, represents far larger bets, a much greater flow of gambling cash. If policy, an estimated $1.5 billion racket, can pour so many millions out in "ice," what must bookmaking, an estimated $3-$5 billion racket, pay? When one begins to add the two "pads" together, one begins to comprehend, if only dimly, the almost total corruption of law enforcement and society that has been the prime achievement of the underworld.

For an insight into bookmaking payoffs, let's turn to an interview with a former New York plainclothesman as recorded by Samuel Dash in *The Eavesdroppers,* a study of wiretapping financed by the Fund for the Republic and published in 1959 by Rutgers University Press. The plainclothesman interviewed by Dash had been on the force between 1947 and 1951, in the days when the Harry Gross ring was operating in Brooklyn. As a result, his figures on police "ice" are somewhat out of date, but "the system" he described is unchanged today.

This plainclothesman explained that illegal wiretapping was a general practice. Sleuths, he said, were always on the lookout for a bookie trying to sneak a play without a payoff—not, however, so that they could arrest him, but so that they could shake him down. Discovery of a character so stupid as to try to dodge the payoff, the plainclothesman pointed out, "could be worth anywhere from $500 to $1,000 to me personally." He added that, if you were lucky enough to grab a bookie's work sheets, you could really shake him down because, if he lost those sheets, everybody who bet with him that day would claim that they won, and the poor man would be ruined. "He has no way of knowing who plays what, and you put him out of business," the former plainclothesman pointed out. "Then all he can do is pay everybody. So it's cheaper to pay you."

Q. How extensive is that practice?

A. Oh, let me say that any man who is susceptible and needs an extra dollar will do it.

Q. And would that be true of most plainclothesmen?

A. I don't like to say this because I like being a policeman, but I think it's true of almost every cop. I don't say all. . . . There are a number who will do it and do it continuously. The average fellow will take a bribe of say $5 to $10 and he worries about it for six years later. That's the average policeman. I know some and believe me I know quite a few who wouldn't touch a nickel if you forced it into their pockets. Unfortunately, those men are out in uniform on the street, and they're not where they have the opportunity of taking anything. But it's a terrible temptation to a man who makes, I'll say, $80 a week and he's walking around with $1.50 in his pockets and he knows his wife has $3 to run the house for four days and somebody else has $500 just to walk away with just a piece of paper in his pocket.

Q. To what extent is this practice known by the supervisor of police personnel?

A. Well, let me put it this way. A telephone costs [a bookie] $1,500.

Q. To get a telephone in?

A. No, to keep a telephone would cost you approximately $1,500 a month. And that had to be divided all the way down the line. The division plainclothesmen realized about $10 of that $1,500 individually. Now if you have ten plainclothesmen—now that's $100—that goes for the ten plainclothesmen. Well, believe it or not, that's the ratio. Then you have a lieutenant in charge. First you have the two "shooflies." They're supervisors in plainclothes. They could be a lieutenant, they could be a sergeant. They have to be cut in for a share. The borough office has to go in. His boss has to go in—it goes right up the line.

All the evidence indicates that the price of protection has grown steadily more exorbitant with the passage of years. More millions are being poured into gambling now than was the case ten years ago, and inevitably the size of the "pad" has increased.

No longer can a bookmaker in New York City obtain an "okay phone," meaning complete protection on every echelon of the Police Department, for a mere $1,500 a month. A couple of years ago, one veteran of the profession asserted that the going rate was $2,000 a month for each phone, each "spot" in the city—and that there were at least 500 "spots" operating under this system. Since that time, the bite on policy operators has mounted to a minimum of $2,500 a month, and it is logical to assume that the bookies, who handle an even heavier cash business, do not escape the greedy grasp of a corrupted law any more lightly.

Let's see what kind of a price tag this places on over-all corruption. Even if one assumes that the 150 books who appeared on the Tollin code list were the only ones operating in the city, an "okay phone" costing each book $2,500 a month would pyramid to a monthly pay-off of

$375,000—a yearly take of $4.5 million. If there were 500 books operating in the five boroughs with their eight million population, a figure that is considered ultra-conservative in the trade, the annual graft from bookmaking alone would mount to $15 million. And when one adds to this the policy "pad," one comes to the almost inevitable conclusion that corruption in New York is probably a $20 million annual business.

No one supposes that the police are allowed to wallow by themselves in this happy mire. As the ex-Brooklyn plainclothesman told Dash, "It goes right up the line," and inevitably a sizeable hunk must be diverted into political coffers. If it weren't, the politicians, who after all do control the city government and the police and all the other agencies of law enforcement, wouldn't permit the system to operate for a minute. But this "system" has endured for decades now, it still goes on, practically everybody knows about it—and nobody does anything to stop it.

6

YOU CAN'T HELP THE LAW

THE underworld's gambling billions wield such influence on both politics and the police that law enforcement in many vital areas in America is literally beyond help. It is so far gone down the trail of bribery and connivance that even when its nose is rubbed in the scent of its quarry it smells no scent and it catches nothing.

This determined insensitivity of the law is widely apparent, but perhaps nowhere more glaring than in certain sensitive fiefs outside Chicago in the North and New Orleans in the South. Just across the Chicago city line, in Cicero, Illinois, the heirs of Al Capone run a gambling barony that has defied time and repeated exposure. In Jefferson Parish, just outside New Orleans, the Carlos Marcello mob, its activities thoroughly aired by the Kefauver Committee ten years ago, flourishes as if the Kefauver exposé had never been.

What makes both of these mob operations especially noxious is that they are being conducted in areas served by two of the most dedicated crime commissions in the nation—the Chicago Crime Commission, directed by Virgil W. Peterson, a nationally recognized expert on the ties and activities of the underworld, and the Metropolitan Crime Commission of New Orleans, whose managing director is Aaron M. Kohn, a former aide of J. Edgar Hoover.

The crime commissions of both cities, in the face of official sloth and indifference, have time after time uncovered evidence of wide-open gambling that seems otherwise invisible to the eyes of the law; both have adopted the forthright tactic of giving agencies of the law specific information, so detailed as to names, times, and places that it would seem inaction would be impossible; and both have seen these factual data deliberately and repeatedly ignored.

Peterson and the Chicago Crime Commission investigators pressed a persistent campaign beginning in August, 1956, to make the law aware of determined efforts by syndicate boss Tony Accardo to reopen the multi-million-dollar gambling operations that had flourished previously at such sites as Ralph's Place, The Fort, and the Trot Inn. Cook County Sheriff at the time was Joseph D. Lohman, a former University of Chicago professor, criminologist of note, and consultant to police departments throughout the nation. Peterson detailed plans of the Chicago syndicate to open a big gambling house on West Gunnison Street, and Lohman initially acted on this information. He raided the place and made several arrests, but then his interest lapsed. As Peterson later reported, the big game subsequently opened on the very premises that had been raided, ran there for a few weeks, and then moved to Cicero, long a hotbed of Capone mob activity. The Chicago commission noted that the town "continued to furnish a friendly atmosphere for syndicate gambling places in 1956. At least one gang killing in 1956 stemmed from Cicero gambling operations."

In 1957, the Chicago Crime Commission concentrated on wide-open gambling in Cicero. During the year it sent nine letters to the sheriff's office containing specific details on Cicero gambling operations. One huge game had run at the same site for more than ten years; the address and the operators had been publicly identified during the Kefauver probe—yet nothing had changed, the gambling spot ran wide open right where it had always been.

"Each letter listed from eight to fourteen addresses where Crime Commission investigators found gambling in operation." Peterson wrote later. "Several raids were made by the Sheriff's office, but many of the places soon resumed operations in the friendly climate that seems to prevail for Cicero gamblers year after year. . . . One address was reported in eight of [the letters], two addresses in seven, one in six, and another in four. And with reference to these five addresses, from April 11, 1952, through 1957, the Chicago Crime Commission has reported one address 63 times, another 59 times, another 52 times, another 51 times and still another 50 times.

"The persistent character of Cicero gambling establishments is illustrated by Joseph Corngold's place at 5914 West Cermak Road, Cicero, Ill. This address was reported in Chicago Crime Commission letters to the Sheriff's office eight times in 1957. When Capone gang leader Louis (Little New York) Campagna appeared before the Kefauver U.S. Senate Committee in 1950, he testified that he had been in partnership with Joseph Corngold and Willie Heeney in the operation of two gambling places in Cicero called the El Patio, at 5914 West Cermak Road, and the Austin Club located at Roosevelt Road and Austin Boulevard. Campagna testified that this partnership was started in 1934 and his share of the earnings amounted to $75,000 a year. Campagna and Heeney are both deceased, but Corngold and the gambling place at 5914 West Cermak Road appear to go on forever with the blessing of Cicero officials."

They went on in 1958 as if the Chicago Crime Commission had not spoken so bluntly in 1957. Obviously, officials in Cicero and Cook County, if they could read, were not practicing the art; but the Crime Commission continued to direct specific reports about gambling to Sheriff Lohman's office. It sent the Sheriff seven letters pinpointing eighty-two gambling spots. In a letter dated October 22, 1958, the commission commented acidly:

"Many of the gambling places set forth have been known to your office for a number of years. Yet the places continue to operate without fear of raids or arrests."

One of these became involved in headline disclosures that caused an unaccustomed flush of embarrassment to rise to the cheeks of certain public officials. A major Capone syndicate crap game was clicking along merrily in an air-conditioned room in the rear of the Viaduct Lounge at 4612 West Cermak Road—not far from the famed Corngold game. As early as August, 1956, the commission had identified the proprietors as Rocco Fischetti, Leslie Kruse, Gus Liebe, and Johnny Drew—"all well-known, big time syndicate gambling operators," the commission said in a November, 1956, letter. "As we have informed you in earlier communications, we are confident that a properly conducted raid on this operation around 11:30 at night, particularly on Friday or Saturday, would net top-notch Capone syndicate gambling house operators . . . I am sure you will agree with us that it is disgraceful for this place to operate. . . . We feel confident that you can put this place out of business permanently. . . . The profits to the Capone syndicate are enormous."

The law took no effective action; the game continued to run. Then on July 7, 1958, the *Chicago Tribune* sent reporters George Bliss and Sandy Smith to the West Cermak Road address to see what they could see. They saw plenty and reported all in a story that the *Tribune* displayed prominently. The two reporters identified August J. (Gus) Liebe as the manager of the game. Liebe had talked frankly to them. The game, he said, was "too big to hide," and he added frankly: "There is no such thing as sneaking with a big gambling operation. It is bound to attract a lot of attention. I guess the Sheriff just doesn't know his way around."

When this newspaper exposé exploded in the face of a startled officialdom, the reaction was ludicrous. As Peterson noted in his 1958 report, "the sheriff's office expressed surprise and indicated a total unfamiliarity with either the location or Liebe!"

This wasn't by any means an isolated or unusual incident. Peterson's commission found gambling running wide open in other towns in the county and kept bombarding Sheriff Lohman with letters listing the names and addresses at which the law was being flouted. An especial target of these warnings was a gambling casino known as the Casa Madrid at 171 North 25th Avenue in Melrose Park. The proprietor was Rocco De Grazzio, a man with important Capone syndicate affiliations. The crime commission, on January 30 and February 25, 1958, wrote Sheriff Lohman that the Casa Madrid "has been a notorious gambling operation for many years and has been known throughout the country as a syndicate gambling joint." The commission urged that a "well-planned and executed" raid be conducted.

Again the warning fell on deaf ears; and again, on July 28, 1958, the *Chicago Tribune* featured a page-one story in which reporters described in minute detail the huge operation flourishing in the Casa Madrid. Even this prominent public exposure wasn't sufficiently potent to stir the law. As Peterson noted: "The place continued to flourish . . . and on November 28, 1958, Illinois State Police officers raided the Casa Madrid, dispersing one hundred persons and arresting six employees of the gambling establishment."

Lohman made some 1,500 gambling and vice raids during his tenure, a show of energy that inspired his supporters to bill him as "the best sheriff Cook County ever had" in calm disregard of the fact that the prize enterprises of the Capone mob had suffered little interference.

In 1959 Lohman swept on to bigger and better things as State Treasurer of Illinois, and the vacant law-enforcement position was occupied by Frank G. Sain. One of Sain's first acts was to appoint Chicago Police Captain Thomas Harrison head of Cook County Highway Police. Harrison had once been discharged from the Chicago police force on charges of failing to suppress gambling in his district, but had appealed in the courts and won reinstatement. Subsequently, in testimony before the Kefauver Committee, he had admitted that in 1937 he had received a gift of $32,500 from a gambling racketeer. Discharged again by the Civil Service Commission, Harrison again fought the verdict in the courts, won a split-decision reversal from the Illinois Supreme Court, once more was reinstated. As Peterson noted: "With this background . . . the appointment of Captain Thomas Harrison as head of the Cook County Highway Police is hardly one to inspire confidence of more effective enforcement of the gambling laws of Cicero, Melrose Park, and other parts of the county." Nevertheless, the Chicago Crime Commission continued to share their discoveries with the law—and with no better results than in the past.

A letter on April 22, 1959, described sixteen gambling

spots. Five were in Calumet Park, and one of the most important of these was described: "12900 South Ashland Avenue, Calumet Park, Ill., Club Corral—Commercial casino gambling . . . operated in a rear room of this place. Cars are parked within a stockade at the rear and attendants supervise the admission of known patrons into the gambling room through the back door entrance covered with a canopy. This is a syndicate night-time operation and is going full blast about 1 or 2 in the morning."

The result?

"Big casino gambling operations continued to flourish in the place until late in July," Peterson reported sadly. "At that time a feature story written by George Bliss of the *Chicago Tribune* focused public attention on the plush gambling establishment still flourishing in the Club Corral."

Publicity doesn't mean much for the mob when it does not have to worry about the one thing that matters—the law. The public forgets, and the gamblers, as the wisecracking Willie Moretti once boasted, "just fade and fade." This truth was clearly illustrated in the destinies of the Viaduct Lounge and the Casa Madrid. Despite exposure and embarrassment, despite an occasional raid, they continued to run and run.

In his report at the end of the year Peterson described what the Chicago Crime Commission had been attempting to accomplish in the face of massive official lethargy:

"On January 15, 1959, the Crime Commission reported nineteen establishments including the Casa Madrid in Melrose Park, Ill., a persistent Capone syndicate violator for many years, an establishment in Stickney owned and operated by Al Capone's brother, the old Wagonwheel operation in Norwood Park Township in which

Sam (Mooney) Giancana has had a lucrative interest for many years, and numerous places in Cicero. . . ."

Some of the establishments in this locality also specialized in vice. In a letter to the sheriff's office on January 21, 1959, the Crime Commission reported several Cicero places in which gambling was flourishing, and in three of them vice was also present. Strip-tease girls were giving obscene performances completely in the nude, while 'B' girls were soliciting for prostitution as well as for drinks.

"Over a period of many years the Chicago Crime Commission has reported a highly lucrative Capone syndicate crap game that has operated in various sections of Cook County and for a time in Lake County, Ill. In recent years this game has operated at 4612 West Cermak Road in Cicero, Ill. [Here Peterson repeated the details of the November, 1956, letter to the sheriff's office in which he had named the proprietors of the Viaduct Lounge and urged a raid.] Yet almost three years elapsed before the first effective action was taken on September 5, 1959. And this action was taken by the office of State's Attorney Benjamin S. Adamowski and not by local Cicero officials or the Sheriff's office, which had primary responsibility for law enforcement in Cicero.

"On September 5, 1959, representatives of the State's Attorney's office conducted a well-planned and executed raid on the Viaduct Lounge located at 4612 West Cermak Road in Cicero. Among those seized by the State's Attorney's investigators were Rocco Fischetti, cousin of Al Capone and a powerful gambling king in Cook County for many years, Gus Liebe, manager of Capone syndicate casino gambling establishments for decades, and Leslie Kruse, who together with Capone gang leader Tony Accardo has operated the infamous Owl Club in Calumet

City, Ill. Others arrested in the establishment included a nationally known boxing racketeer and gambler who has been active principally in the East. It will be noted that in large part the identical Capone gang bigwigs listed in the Crime Commission letter of November 2, 1956, as operating the establishment . . . were arrested by the State's Attorney's investigators as managers of the place when it was raided on September 5, 1959. Also seized in the raid were bundles of currency totaling $89,284.75.

"Officials responsible for enforcing the law should be held strictly accountable for the performance of their sworn duties," Peterson angrily concluded. "If they continue to show no inclination to perform their sworn duty they should be charged with nonfeasance or malfeasance. . . . It is time that drastic action be taken against responsible officials who persistently refuse to enforce the laws in the public interest."

When he wrote this, Peterson's disposition had been further soured by an open display of affection between Tony Accardo and Lieutenant Anthony De Grazio, of the Chicago police. In late October, 1959, Accardo took his wife on a tour of Europe; accompanying them were Lieutenant De Grazio and his wife. This rapport between Chicago's number one gangster and a lieutenant on the Chicago police force made news around the world. The publicity left Lieutenant De Grazio considerably miffed. He pointed out that Accardo had been an usher at his wedding in 1927, and when Accardo was married in 1934, De Grazio, then a sergeant, had accompanied the gang leader and his bride on their honeymoon. Besides, Lieutenant De Grazio wondered righteously, what was wrong about associating with Tony Accardo? He had never been convicted of anything.

This last statement accorded perfectly with the facts. Tony Accardo had been accused of almost every conceivable crime—forgery, perjury, tax cheating, hijacking, bootlegging, robbery, kidnaping, extortion, gambling, narcotics peddling, labor racketeering, pandering, and murder. But the worst that had ever happened to him was a $200 fine for disorderly conduct. True, he had been relieved of the necessity of going into the armed forces in World War II because his River Forest draft board had found him "morally unfit for military service," but what might make a man morally unfit for army associations obviously didn't disqualify him, in Lieutenant De Grazio's view, to be the bosom friend of a member of the Chicago police force.

The foreign travels of the gangster and the cop kicked up a temporary tempest, but this wasn't the worst of the trouble that was brewing for Tony Accardo in 1959. Milton Wessel's Midwest rackets-busting team had its eye on him, and three special Justice Department prosecutors—Richard B. Ogilvie, William B. Carey, and Walter D. Cummings—began to subject Accardo's income tax returns to minute scrutiny. Accardo's enormous income for years had been no secret. For a man who had spent most of his life without honest vocation, he had prospered exceedingly well. He lived in a 22-room mansion with gold-plated plumbing, set on spacious grounds behind a six-foot high iron fence electrically wired to discourage intrusion. The estate was valued at half a million dollars and was located at 915 Franklin Avenue in the exclusive River Forest section of Chicago.

The source of this affluence had stirred the curiosity of investigators in the past, and both the Kefauver and McClellan committees had exposed Accardo's sources of income. They showed, for example, that Accardo and Jack

Guzik had divided between them $278,000 from the profits of a single South Side policy wheel in 1949. During the same period, 1948 and 1949, Accardo had been sharing in the take of the notorious Owl Club, which grossed about $2 million in horse-race bets alone in those two years. In 1958 the federal government tried to collect an additional $90,565 in taxes from Accardo on his Owl Club profits, but the U.S. Tax Court in Washington drastically reduced the claim in conformity with a Supreme Court decision that gangsters must be allowed, like any legitimate businessmen, to deduct the expenses of operating their illicit enterprises. As a result Tony Accardo continued to enjoy immunity from the law until the three Midwest federal rackets-busters started on his trail.

They began to probe into a tax dodge that enabled Accardo to report—and pay taxes on—a heavy, seemingly legitimate income. In 1956, 1957, and 1958, Accardo listed himself as "a sales promotion man" for Premium Beer Sales Inc. He reported and paid taxes on an income of $179,273 for the three years. In doing so, he had claimed as "a business expense" an item of $3,993, or 90 per cent of the cost of operating his fire-engine red Mercedes sports car. Government prosecutors based their attack on Accardo on the premise that the entire whopping salary from Premium was a device to give him so much "legitimate" spending money that it would be almost impossible to develop an income tax fraud case against him. It was the government's contention that Accardo had never sold a can of beer and that, when he charged off his sports car expenses to the beer business, he was committing a clear fraud.

Hardly had the federal probe begun, when murder came in its train. On July 19, 1959, Joseph Bronge, 50, a beer distributor, was gunned down and mortally wounded by two killers after he had been indicted for perjury for refusing to tell whether gangsters had "muscled" their way onto his payroll. And on January 20, 1960, Arthur Adler, 44, who had been questioned before a federal grand jury about alleged gangster ownership of cafés, disappeared. His body was found weeks later stuffed into a West Side sewer. Despite these setbacks federal prosecutors continued to build the case against Accardo. In April, 1960, he was indicted on three counts of federal income tax evasion, and in November he was convicted by a jury. Judge Julius Hoffman threw the book at Accardo, sentencing him to six years in prison, fining him $15,000, and assessing him for the full costs of the nine-week jury trial—a penalty that, attorneys said, would be astronomical.

In imposing sentence, Judge Hoffman charged that Accardo had dealt "in degradation and violence," and added: "The only conclusion we can draw from the huge amounts of income from professional gambling which permeates all levels of society is that organized gambling is a malignancy and a national calamity."

Accardo announced at once that he would appeal. In the meantime, it appeared that the reins of Chicago gangdom would pass into the ready and waiting hands of Sam (Mooney) Giancana.

If the Accardo verdict stands, it will be the first time that the acknowledged chief of Chicago gangdom has ever viewed the world from the wrong side of prison bars. Up to this time Accardo, at 54, has outdone his colleague Joe Adonis in long-term immunity, and it is significant that nothing more serious than a parking ticket or a disorderly conduct fine ever happened to either of them until federal exposures brought upon their heads the wrath of belated justice. It is notable, too, that in Accardo's case this was solely the achievement of federal law and a federal rackets-busting team—definitely not that of the local law.

This is a pattern that by now has become sickeningly familiar. The frustrating experiences of Virgil Peterson and his Chicago Crime Commission have been duplicated almost step by step in New Orleans by those of Aaron Kohn and his Metropolitan Crime Commission. In New Orleans, Kohn has been trying to fight the criminal empire of an equally unlovely thug, as unlovely as Tony Accardo—Carlos Marcello, reputed head of the Mafia in Louisiana and now a "legitimate" businessman and multi-millionaire.

Born Calorso Minicari in Tunis, North Africa, on February 6, 1910, the son of Sicilian parents, Carlos Marcello was brought to this country when he was eight months old. His police record began November 29, 1929, when he was nineteen. He and his brother Peter, then seventeen, were arrested as accessories to a bank robbery in the Algiers section of New Orleans. The verdict of the law was to become a familiar refrain in Marcello's career—charges dismissed.

Marcello's further police dossier is dotted with entries, sometimes cryptic and vague, and usually fading away into nothingness. As Kohn pieced it together before the McClellan rackets committee, it reads like this:

May 13, 1930—On this date, just six months after his first offense, Carlos Marcello was convicted of assault and robbery and sentenced to serve 9 to 14 years in the state penitentiary. He was paroled on September 12, 1934.

January 7, 1935—At liberty barely four months, he was charged with assault and robbery of $20 from a grocery store in New Orleans, and with assault, beating and wounding with intent to murder Robert P. Childress, an employee of the New Orleans Police Department. Both charges were dropped.

February 17, 1935—Picked up for violation of U.S. Internal Revenue laws, charge dismissed on May 2, 1935.

July 25, 1935—Despite the two interim charges casting doubt on his reformation, Marcello was granted a full pardon in the assault and robbery case that had sent him to prison. Governor O. K. Allen, a stooge of Huey Long's, granted the pardon. Coincidentally, Frank Costello and his partner, "Dandy Phil" Kastel, were setting up their slot machine empire in Louisiana with Long's connivance—and Marcello was part of their combine, the first indication in his career of top-level racket ties.

June, 1938—Marcello was charged with selling marijuana to a man with a record as a previous narcotics violator. The purchaser was sent back to prison for parole violation, but charges against Marcello were dismissed.

September 8, 1938—Marcello and another man, a narcotics violator, were picked up by New Orleans police after a high-speed chase through city streets. They were arrested coming out of a vacant lot in which a discarded gun was found. Official records give no hint of what disposition was made of this case.

October 29, 1938—On this date Marcello pleaded guilty to selling more than twenty-three pounds of untaxed marijuana. He had been picked up some months earlier by federal agents in what was described at the time as a roundup of "the biggest marijuana ring in New Orleans' history," and he had been out on bail on this charge when he acquired the June and September notations on his record. He was committed to the federal penitentiary in Atlanta and fined $76,830.

August 18, 1939—Marcello was discharged from Atlanta Penitentiary after serving nine and one-half months on the narcotics rap. That $76,830 fine was a bit of a problem, but Marcello found a way to deal with it. His wife filed an affidavit asserting that they were insolvent—$1,409 in debt—and that her only income was $50 a month from a small liquor store. Though Marcello already had high mob contacts through Costello and Kastel and was quite a local bigshot, the law evidently believed his wife's poverty plea; for Marcello, once out of prison, settled the $76,830 federal lien for just $400.

October, 1940—U. S. Immigration agents evidently discovered Marcello was an alien who had never bothered to become naturalized; also, he was arrested by New Orleans police for having no honest means of support. Both charges faded.

January 13, 1948—A newspaper photographer charged that Marcello and a bodyguard had grabbed and destroyed his camera and films, then had backed him up against a wall and had gone through his pockets. The incident happened in front of the Gretna Green Court House, in the presence of deputy sheriffs who watched and did nothing. The photographer had been taking pictures of demonstrators protesting the sheriff's interference with a political parade. Charges were filed against Marcello and bodyguard; disposition—another blank.

January 25, 1951—On the witness stand before the Kefauver Committee, Marcello balked at questions regarding his financial interest in the Jefferson Music Company, the Dixie Coin Machine Company, bars, restaurants, night clubs, slot machines, pinball games, juke boxes, gambling casinos, a horse-race-betting wire service, a taxicab company, oil fields, a shrimp fishery, a frozen food packaging plant. The far-ranging questions indicated vividly how wealthy the "pauper" of 1939 had become in a little more than eleven years.

January 17, 1955—Horace Perez, a notorious gambler and associate of Marcello, went on trial for bribery. State Police Major-Inspector Aaron Edgecombe had laid the trap; several thousand dollars Perez had paid him to buy protection for gambling in Marcello's private fief, Jefferson Parish, were introduced into evidence. Wire-tapped recordings of conversations with Perez were read to the jury. Perez was convicted. He and an associate were later convicted of a similar bribery attempt in Orleans Parish. But the following year the late Governor Earl Long pardoned the pair, and after the pardon, *the courts ruled that the marked graft money must be returned to the convicted bribers.*

Here one finds again the virtual triumph of the underworld over the forces of law. It may be argued that Louisiana, a state with a long tradition of corruption by gambling millions, represents a loaded case. Perhaps. But it must be remembered that New York has had its Frank Costello; New Jersey, its Joe Adonis; Chicago, its Tony Accardo; Las Vegas and California, their Buggsy Siegel and Jack Dragna and Mickey Cohen; Florida and New York, the Meyer and Jake Lanskys—just to mention a few. Some of these have weathered all exposures and are still in power. As a rule, nothing has ever happened to any of these crime lords unless they (1) double-crossed their own syndicate brethren and got knocked off—like Buggsy Siegel, or (2) had the bad luck to run into sensational exposures like Kefauver's—events that create such a hullabaloo that something simply has to be done.

But even such outcries are usually unproductive of real or lasting results. The underworld, having made its few essential sacrifices to the law, runs on and on, pyramiding its wealth and infiltrating legitimate business until it has become almost impossible to tell where racket ends and business begins. This is done in open defiance of every level of law enforcement in America, right up to the highest federal level. Anyone who doubts this need only to examine the charmed life Carlos Marcello has led in the ten years since Kefauver exposed him.

First U.S. Immigration authorities attempted to deport Marcello. Racket bosses commanding the millions that hire slick legal mouthpieces always make this a long-drawn-out process, but Marcello was a champion of delay. He was an alien with a long criminal record, including sentences for assault and robbery and narcotics, yet ever since 1952 he has kept the federal government tied in knots in the courts and has defied every effort to boot him back to Tunis. All that has happened, as Aaron Kohn made clear in his testimony before the McClellan committee in 1959, is that Marcello has grown infinitely more wealthy and more powerful; he and his mob virtually dominate Jefferson Parish, the gambling mecca to the west and south of New Orleans.

The cornerstone of Marcello's empire was laid as early as 1940 in the Jefferson Music Company, located at 335 Huey P. Long Avenue, Gretna, Louisiana. In those days of Marcello's alleged pauperism, the company was operated in the name of his mother, Mrs. Louise Marcello, but in January, 1942, she transferred title to Carlos' younger brother Vincent, still a minor at the time. The business listed 49 slot machines, 50 music boxes, 62 pinball games, and other equipment at 84 different locations, mostly in the Algiers section of New Orleans. In 1944, Carlos Marcello's interest in Jefferson Music came into the open when he and Vincent formed a partnership. Within two years, each was drawing $25,000 annually from the company.

As Carlos Marcello's business interests grew, his younger brothers took over the operation of Jefferson Music; but Carlos, according to the Metropolitan Crime Commission, still makes his headquarters there, finding it a handy rendezvous for meeting racketeers and politicians. Significantly, the expenses of his legal battle against deportation have been charged off to Jefferson Music. His continuing close ties to the firm became highly relevant in 1957 when the scandal-riddled Federal Communications Commission granted Jefferson Music a license to operate a citizens' radio station, authorizing installation of thirteen transmitters of the kind used in automobiles and other vehicles. Aaron Kohn and the Metropolitan Crime Commission filed a vigorous but futile protest. They pointed out that under the law it was illegal to issue such a license to an alien; that Jefferson Music itself always had been in the illegal slot machine business; that Marcello's associates still ran an illegal horse-race wire service of inestimable aid to Louisiana bookmakers; and that, in effect, an FCC radio license was no boon for the federal government to bestow upon a ring so blatantly involved in illegality.

None of these arguments seemed to register with the FCC. Carlos Marcello's old firm got its license without difficulty. The extent of his power was demonstrated in the activities of a couple of other companies—the Huey Distributing Company, 3760 Airline Highway, Jefferson Parish, and the Vac-Key Amusement Company at the same address. Both firms dealt in jukeboxes and pinball machines. According to Kohn and the Metropolitan Crime Commission, within weeks after Sheriff William S. Coci took office in Jefferson Parish in June, 1956, two of his deputy sheriffs began calling at the busier bars and restaurants, ordering them to remove their jukeboxes and install those being distributed by the two Marcello companies. "Put in our machines, or we'll close up your handbook," the deputies allegedly told one proprietor. Needless to say, the new machines—even though they played only three records for a quarter instead of the usual single play for a nickel and gave the businesses where they were installed a smaller percentage—soon became popular in joints all over Jefferson Parish.

The jukebox, pinball, and slot machine companies represented just one tiny tributary in the enormous river of Carlos Marcello's wealth. Gambling of every sort furnished him with millions with which he expanded into all kinds of legitimate enterprises. Indicative of his fiscal and criminal stature in 1946, just seven years after he had pleaded abject poverty before the federal government, Marcello bought a 17 per cent interest in the Beverly Club for $45,000—cash. The Beverly Club, in which Frank Costello and "Dandy Phil" Kastel were principal stockholders, was one of the most lavish night clubs and gambling casinos in the nation. It did a multi-million-dollar annual business and ran for years until the Kefauver investigation caused a temporary rash of conscience on the part of the law. With the proceeds of the Beverly Club flowing into his coffers, Marcello and an associate in May, 1948, put up $160,000 to purchase the New Southport Club, a gambling casino in Jefferson Parish.

Gambling millions flowed in from all these enterprises, and Carlos Marcello plowed the money into many fields—into real estate, oil wells, bars and restaurants and motels, the Louisiana Quick Freeze and Storage Company, and the Sea Shrimp Company, operating trawlers in the Gulf of Mexico. Though the Kefauver probe temporarily pinched off the revenue from his flossy gambling casinos such as the Beverly Club, Marcello's other enterprises flourished. In 1958 he and his five brothers, two sisters, and mother sold a 183-acre tract in Gretna for just a penny less than $1 million. In July of the same year the million-dollar-plus Town & Country Motel opened at Rossier City near Shreveport—an enterprise in which Marcello's attorney and business partners appeared as principal stockholders. A third transaction in 1958 gave Marcello a substantial interest in the Holiday Inn Hotel in Jefferson Parish, purchased for $1.8 million. These were not by any means the only transactions but merely three selected at random to indicate the enormous wealth and power the rackets had placed in the hands of the one-time punk.

An essential concomitant of racket power is political power; as the Massachusetts Crime Commission noted, it is fair to say one cannot exist without the other. Marcello's political influence has been demonstrated on many occasions, but perhaps never more graphically than in the favoritism he has been shown on the tax-assessment rolls of Jefferson Parish. His former home in Marrero, Louisiana, acquired in 1946 for $42,500 and advertised for sale in 1959 for $125,000, was carried on the tax rolls at an assessment of $8,000. The New Southport Club, the gambling casino he bought in 1948 for $160,000, was assessed at $7,200. The Town & Country Motel in Jefferson Parish, built in 1953 at a cost of $350,000 and offered for sale by Marcello in 1959 for more than $1 million, was assessed at just $17,500. It goes without saying that the ordinary citizen, who often pays exorbitant taxes on his home, is rarely treated with such infinite consideration by the tax authorities.

The Metropolitan Crime Commission has compiled a

list of the prominent racket, business, and political figures who have been identified attending Marcello's court in the dilapidated and sinister Willswood Tavern. Located across the Mississippi from New Orleans, bordered by marshes and isolated from prying eyes, the tavern has past associations with narcotics peddling and murder. Marcello, though he has many more lavish conference sites at his disposal, apparently still retains a fondness for the privacy of the dilapidated Willswood.

Attending some of his meettings there, according to the crime commission, have been such distinguished figures as Sheriff Coci and Charles Spencer, president of Jefferson Parish. The commission has also spotted another curious tie with Jefferson Parish officials in the ownership of Marcello's elaborate weekend retreat in the village of Grand Isle on the Gulf of Mexico. His property there is registered in the name of Philip B. Smith, Attorney for Jefferson Parish, appointed to that post by Spencer.

Against this background it is not exactly surprising to find that Aaron Kohn and the Metropolitan Crime Commission, even with the aid of repeated exposés in the New Orleans press, have not been able to put the slightest dent in Marcello's racket empire. The kind of supreme power a racketeer can wield can be understood only when one appreciates the comparative ease with which a man like Marcello has turned aside persistent efforts to persuade, pressure and embarrass the law into action.

From 1956 the Metropolitan Crime Commission has followed the same technique Virgil Peterson uses in Chicago. It has made its own investigations, uncovered its own evidence, and furnished responsible officials ranging from Sheriff Coci to the governor with details of law violations. It has issued public statements exposing both lawbreaking and the inaction of the law. In a formal resolution passed on September 27, 1956, the commission noted that it had notified Sheriff Coci of law violations at twenty-seven locations in Jefferson Parish. These included every kind of gambling—handbook, roulette, dice, cards, pinballs, lotteries, and punchboards; and they included, too, other crimes such as prostitution, liquor-law violations, liquor sales to juveniles, gambling by juveniles. Having failed to get action, the commission called on the District Attorney, the Superintendent of State Police, and Governor Long to act. Nobody in Louisiana became excited.

In the next two years, the commission returned to the attack again and again. It was greatly helped by the local press. In one sensational series of articles in early June, 1957, the New Orleans *States* sent veteran crime reporter Edwin Strickland into Jefferson Parish. Strickland, on loan from the Birmingham *News*, had covered the Phenix City vice and corruption scandal, and he drew a deadly parallel between the conditions that had been exposed in Alabama's "City of Sin" and those he found in Jefferson Parish. He discovered that the Kefauver exposé had simply made Jefferson Parish mobsters more secretive and cautious; they stopped operating huge and blatant gambling casinos like the Beverly Club and the New Southport Club. But every other kind of gambling racket flourished, with the open connivance of authorities.

In a series of articles Strickland proclaimed that slot machines had again become a multi-million-dollar racket, that bookmaking was operated so openly that results from the tracks were announced over loud-speaking systems, that dice and gambling games of every kind flourished. He wrote:

"I have seen horse bets placed and openly discussed

while a policeman sat drinking a cup of coffee almost within arm's reach of the bookie.

"I have seen Sheriff's deputies in Jefferson Parish in places where the clang of the slot machines almost drowned out conversation.

"I've even had a policeman kibitz while I played and made a hit on a horse-racing machine and was paid off over the counter."

Sheriff Coci's response to this was to call Strickland and the New Orleans *States* "liars." He said he had had his deputies check 300 establishments for slot and horse-race machines—and had found nothing. In the wake of this official action Jefferson Parish, according to the Metropolitan Crime Commission, went happily back to its gambling ways.

Murder, as it almost always does, followed in gambling's train. On January 25, 1958, a notorious gambler was gunned down almost on the steps of The Ranch, a barroom that the Metropolitan Crime Commission had repeatedly named to Sheriff Coci. In an angry telegram to the Sheriff, Aaron Kohn exploded:

"You have chosen to consistently ignore specific reports and allegations while these criminal activities have continued and expanded. It was inevitable that crimes of violence should arise in this atmosphere of lawlessness which provides a growing sense of immunity from control to those engaged in the ruthlessness of syndicated crime. An objective evaluation of conditions during the past two years leads to the inescapable conclusion that racketeers and hoodlums in Jefferson Parish have been unhampered and encouraged by your office in their achievement of economic and lawless power which now parallels the conditions exposed by the Kefauver Committee in January,

1951. . . . We again call to your attention, as we did last year, laws of our state which describe as a crime the deliberate failure of a public official to perform his duties."

In March, 1959, Kohn took the witness stand before the McClellan committee and put on the record his charges against the Marcello mob and the wide-open gambling in Jefferson Parish. The District Attorney ordered a grand jury probe, the result was another zero, and the crime commission charged that this had been achieved through the failure to call important witnesses. In January and May, 1959, the commission confronted the New Orleans police with evidence of heavy gambling in the city; in July, in another communication to Sheriff Coci, it returned to the attack on Jefferson Parish, stressing that conditions remained unchanged in spite of public revelations before the McClellan committee.

The commission named names, gave addresses. It declared that the Chesterfield Club, which temporarily had ceased operations, was reopened; that the Keyhole Club in Westwego, whose contents had been acquired by Carlos Marcello in a sheriff's sale in 1951, didn't bother to suspend even for an instant the activities of its roaring gambling casino, featuring roulette, dice, blackjack, and keno. The commission identified an entire chain of gambling joints in Jefferson Parish and wrote:

"Perhaps the most heavily trafficked gambling joint in the State is Lambert's Owl Club at 809 Causeway Boulevard. It has been operating for years, with as many as 500 persons estimated recently as participating at one time in the variety of gambling activities, including lottery. A deputy sheriff often has been reported on the premises. The most casual observation of this place, located just off Jefferson Highway, by any passing law-enforcement officer, should be the basis for suspicion and investigation, in view of the hundreds of automobiles parked under the overpass, and jamming the streets and highways."

All that happened was that the Beverly Club reopened. Elaborate redecoration of the long-closed casino proceeded smoothly throughout the spring of 1959, despite the McClellan Committee furor. "Dandy Phil" Kastel still retained his interest in the club; Carlos Marcello was active in directing the renovation. Kastel proclaimed that the Beverly would be just an innocent "supper club," but the Metropolitan Crime Commission wasn't fooled.

In July, 1959, the television-viewing public of New Orleans was treated to one of the most frank and hard-boiled expressions of the credo of the mob that has ever been put on the air. Peter Hand, a New Orleans bookmaker and politician, faced a panel of local newsmen on WYES-TV, and spelled out the bald facts of life. Hand, who made no secret of his bookmaking past and his close affiliation with the slot machine empire of Costello and Kastel, had served for eight years in the Louisiana Legislature and had been a close friend and supporter of Governor Earl Long since 1927. Having viewed the rackets and politics from both sides of the fence, he qualified as an expert on both counts.

The fireworks began early when Hand was asked about a recent statement in which Governor Long had implied that perhaps a few of the legislators were taking bribes. Hand said he thought the Governor had given the legislators a break by saying only a few.

"They give it the name of 'expense money,' " he said, "but I think 98 per cent of them will take this so-called 'expense money' or whatever you want to call it. If you're not an attorney, it's a bribe. If you are an attorney, it's 'expense money' or something of that sort."

Q. Were you paid or given "expense money" to be for or against some legislation?

A. Absolutely, lots of times.

Q. Did you account for it?

A. Yes, sir.

Q. Then . . . it is not wrong to take it; it's wrong not to—

A. —pay federal income tax on it.

Q. Mr. Hand, if I as a citizen want to have certain legislation passed, how do I go about approaching a member of the legislature in a way which would best assure passage of a bill?

A. Well, get yourself one that—well, get someone who knows the legislators, and, if he's a good man and got pretty good connections up there, he's going to tell you right off the bat, "Now this is going to cost you something, because you know these boys up here has got to live," and from then on you and him get together. . . .

Q. How much would you say as a minimum it would cost to get a bill through?

A. Well, it depends upon how large the bill is, and for what big concern and things like that. It may cost you from $500 up.

Q. You make it sound as though—you said 98 per cent of them take this, as you put it, "expense money." Don't you feel that we have any honest legislators at all up there, Mr. Hand?

A. As far as I'm concerned, it's very few. I didn't come across—against any of them, and I served for eight years up there.

The questioning switched to Hand's bookmaking activities. He said quite calmly that he had been a bookmaker for years. But, asked the newsmen, wasn't this illegal?

A. Yes, sir, but you get around that point in certain ways by taking care of certain people.

Q. What do you mean, "certain people?"

A. Well, the law for one, and such things as that. You make a political donation at the proper time and you go on and everything is all right. Nobody will be bothered.

Q. Is it possible to operate a handbook or an illegal gambling game without the consent of the authorities?

A. Absolutely not.

Q. How long could you stay in business—

A. About twenty minutes. You see, today the juke-box operators sent word down the line to all saloon keepers to "buy a federal stamp and you will not be molested by the police," so that shows collusion between the City Hall and the gamblers.

Q. Do you believe the saying, "Every man has his price?"

A. Absolutely. Everybody has a little larceny, grand or petty. You will find that out when you get as old as I am.

Hand was asked about angry trumpetings the State Police Superintendent was making that he was going to "close everything down tight." The veteran bookmaker-politician scoffed. "You will see," he predicted, "around the first of September Jefferson Parish will be open. You see, when a man's governor, he closes them up now and then, and then a little later he sends somebody among the boys and tells them 'reopen.' You will see—in six weeks from now Jefferson will be operating."

He was asked about how widespread gambling was in New Orleans, where it was concentrated.

A. Mostly again in Jefferson, most of your gambling is in Jefferson.

Q. Why is that?

A. Looks like they got the best "fix" up there.

Q. When you say "the best fix," these words sort of startle me, and I am sure they must startle—

A. It don't seem like the Sheriff can find anything wrong out there.

Q. Do you think he is searching?

A. No, I don't think.

The accuracy of Peter Hand's knowledge was indicated by the manner in which his prediction about gambling in Jefferson Parish came true on schedule. On January 13, 1960, Aaron Kohn sent this telegram to Earl Long, then still Governor of Louisiana:

"Current renewal of gambling casino operations at the Beverly Club, Jefferson Highway and Labarre Road, Jefferson Parish, is another flagrant evidence of tolerated organized crime in this area. We urge that the executive powers of your office be invoked through the State Police to promptly suppress the continuing and expanded disdain for state laws by racketeers and law enforcement officers in Jefferson Parish. Details of value to the State Police are available at the Crime Commission office."

Crime and gambling in Louisiana had come full circle. The Beverly Club, the gold mine of Frank Costello, Dandy Phil Kastel, and Carlos Marcello, was roaring wide-open again under the same old sponsorship and in the same old way just as if the Kefauver exposure had never happened.

Nothing drastic happened to the rackets in Jefferson Parish. In an election in 1960, Sheriff Coci was defeated; but as of August, 1960, according to Kohn, "The conditions which were spotlighted by the Kefauver Committee in

January, 1951, remain substantially unsolved." The commission director, reviewing his long and persistent effort "to bring about integrity in law enforcement against organized gambling," added:

"Some progress is achieved by forcing state, parish and municipal officials to retreat from defensive position to defensive position, but they have not yet turned around and made that major lawful assault upon the gambling racketeers which is authorized under the police powers, and which is the only effective governmental means of stopping the flow of illicit wealth into the coffers of such criminals."

When even the most strenuous efforts of dedicated crime commissions can produce from officials only "retreat from defensive position to defensive position," nothing more need be said about the dominance of the rackets—about the almost impregnable grip they have fastened on our political system.

7

LAS VEGAS: GOLDEN PARADISE

WHEN a gunman bounced a bullet off the skull of Frank Costello about 11 P.M., May 2, 1957, the nation was treated to an inadvertent glimpse of the facts of life in Las Vegas, Nevada's monument to human folly, where all gambling is legal—and supposedly pure.

The shooting occurred as Costello entered the lobby of his New York apartment house at 115 Central Park West. The bullet that ploughed a furrow behind his right ear served staccato notice that Costello had been deposed as czar of the New York underworld. It also provided a hint of what lies behind the façade of legality in Nevada.

When Costello was rushed off to a hospital to get his dented head repaired, New York detectives seized the opportunity to go through the contents of his jacket pocket. They found some $800 in cash and a cryptic note dealing with amounts so huge they would have fitted into a page of New York City's annual $2 billion budget. "Gross Casino Win as of 4-26-57 . . . $651,284," the note read, and the total was broken down, "Casino win less markers [that is, I.O.U.s] . . . $434,695. Slot wins $62,844 . . . markers $153,745."

Also recorded on the note were payments: Mike $150

a week, totaling $600; Jake $100 a week, $400; "L—$30,-000, H—$9,000." The note bore the handwriting of two persons.

New York authorities asked Costello to explain what these figures meant. Costello pantomimed amazement that such a weird item could have found its way into his pocket and intimated that he had no idea. Taken before a grand jury, he said most politely and regretfully that he would have to claim the privilege of the Fifth Amendment. Even without his cooperation, however, New York detectives soon established that the note in Costello's pocket represented an accounting on underworld investment in one of the newest and gaudiest casinos to decorate Las Vegas' famous Strip.

The plush Tropicana Hotel had just been opened in Las Vegas. Two of the major stockholders were Chicagoans noted for their political influence, Louis J. Lederer and Charles (Babe) Baron. Baron had headed a Chicago automobile agency, and Lederer had been the secretary of his company. In Las Vegas, Lederer was listed as holding $180,000 worth of Tropicana stock, Baron $120,000, but in the background, from the time the first blueprint was drawn lurked the shadowy figure of "Dandy Phil" Kastel—the slot-machine partner of Frank Costello and the partner of Meyer Lansky and Carlos Marcello in New Orleans' Beverly Club. The Nevada Gaming Control Board had refused to license the Tropicana with Kastel in the picture, and so Kastel obligingly faded a few steps away.

An operating company was formed, called Conquistador, Inc. Kastel signed an agreement relinquishing his interest in the Tropicana. But Conquistador, Inc. was not exactly a free agent; it owed Kastel $320,000, plus other thousands incurred for extra expenses during the hotel's construction, and was obligated to pay off Kastel at a rate of $40,000 a year. Thus, when the hotel opened in April, 1957, with Lederer and Kel Houssels, Sr., in charge of its gambling casino, the Kastel-Costello interest was still there, although half-hidden in the murk of finance.

Less than a month later Costello got himself shot. Authorities compared the note found in his pocket with the gambling returns reported by the new Tropicana and discovered that the two matched, item for item. The Tropicana, in the first twenty-four days of its operation, had reported a gross gambling take of exactly $651,284—not bad for one month's business.

Interestingly enough, the Nevada Gaming Control Board subsequently established that one portion of the note found in Costello's pocket had been written by Michael J. Tanico, a former Tropicana cashier who had been employed previously by Phil Kastel in the Beverly Club. Other portions of the note had been written by Lederer himself; and Lederer was not only connected with the Tropicana, but with another big gambling venture in Las Vegas—that in the Fremont Hotel. So transparent are the links between the most powerful forces in the American underworld and the "legal" gambling that flourishes in Nevada.

Great reams of bilge have been written about what fine characters Nevada's gamblers are and the high plane on which the state's legal racket is run. But the sinister truth is that Nevada's legalization of gambling is one of the greatest boons ever bestowed on the American underworld; the instant the mob discovered what a lovely legal oasis Nevada had made of itself—the only one of its kind in the nation—the masters of syndicate crime in New York and Detroit and Chicago and Cleveland moved in.

The discoverer and first exploiter of this gold mine in the desert was Benjamin (Buggsy) Siegel, co-boss with Meyer Lansky in Prohibition days of New York's infamous "Bug and Meyer" mob of executioners. In the mid-1930's, the "Bug" was sent West as an agent of New York and Chicago syndicates to organize California crime and bring it under the wing of the national cartel. Handsome as a movie star, Buggsy was soon hob-nobbing in exclusive Hollywood circles. George Raft, tough guy of the movies, became a friend and companion. Sponsored by some of the top film executives in Hollywood, Buggsy even wangled himself a membership in exclusive Hillcrest Country Club.

For some years Hollywood didn't appear to realize just what kind of a character it was harboring in dashing Buggsy Siegel. But in 1940 the trail of one fulfilled Murder Inc. contract led Burton Turkus, the principal aide of William O'Dwyer in the Brooklyn District Attorney's office, out to the West Coast and to Buggsy. Invading Buggsy's $200,000, 35-room Holmby Hill palace, complete with swimming pool, Turkus discovered a couple of guns tucked away in a wall safe and, more important than guns, a fascinating set of account books.

These financial ledgers showed that Buggsy, almost from the moment he had arrived in Hollywood, had been systematically shaking down many top film idols. Neatly recorded were "loans" running into four and five figures; none of these "loans" ever had been repaid. One lever Buggsy used to pry such bequests out of movie stars was his power in the movie extras' union. He would simply point out to a star that, unless he or she made a sizable contribution to "the union," the extras would walk off the lot and boycott any picture in which the star was to appear. No extras, no picture—and no future for the star. The stars appreciated the beauty of Buggsy's logic and donated. In one year, Turkus found, their "loans" to Buggsy totaled $400,000.

Handsomely bankrolled by such contributions, Buggsy expanded on all fronts. He brought into his mob organization two of California's most notorious hoods, Jack Dragna and Mickey Cohen. With their aid and in the name of the syndicate, he warred for control of the racing-wire service in the state. It was during this struggle that Buggsy moved into Arizona and Nevada and found waiting for him a golden opportunity.

Gambling had been legalized in Nevada in 1931, but had since been run on a relatively local, small-time basis. Buggsy, who knew all the arts and rewards of big casinos from his association with Meyer Lansky, Joe Adonis and Frank Costello in the East, took a long hard look around in 1942 and decided that Nevada was an untapped treasure chest. First, Buggsy bought into the Golden Nugget and the Frontier Club, two of Las Vegas' busier joints, but such financial adventure only whetted his appetite. A grandiose vision came to him. He would build a fabulous hotel, dedicated to fabulous gambling, right on the three-mile Strip that separates McCarran Airport from Las Vegas. He would call it the Flamingo.

Del Webb, later to become co-owner of the New York Yankees, was the contractor entrusted with the task of turning Buggsy Siegel's dream into reality. So vaulting was Buggsy's vision of the size and appointments of his palace that construction costs ate through even his racket-inflated bankroll. Into the bottomless maw of the Flamingo, Buggsy poured more than $1 million of his own money and at least $5 million of other people's. There is little doubt that a healthy hunk of that extra $5 million came from top-level associates in the syndicate in Chicago and New York.

An anecdote related by a man who advised Buggsy during the erection of the Flamingo speaks volumes about the racket taint in the extravagant hotel. Many millions had been poured into the project, and still the end was not in sight. Regretfully, the adviser broke the news: more money would be needed, thousands of dollars more. Buggsy nodded casually, like a man who has just been told by his wife that he had better get his shirts from the cleaners, and departed on one of his periodic trips to the East.

After an absence of several days, he returned lugging two heavy satchels. Striding into the office of his astonished agent, he grunted with effort as he swung up first one satchel, then the other, plunking his burdens down on the office desk.

"What's this?" the astonished adviser asked.

"Money," said Buggsy. "You said we needed more. Here it is. Let me know if it's not enough."

The satchels were bulging with $400,000 in cash that Buggsy had picked up on his journey. And so the Flamingo was finished.

Buggsy didn't live long to enjoy it. Power went to his head. The evidence indicates that his brother crime czars were not too pleased at the way he had poured their millions into the Flamingo, and their disenchantment with him crystallized when the defiant "Bug" proclaimed he intended to keep all the racket revenues of the West, including that of the race-wire service, strictly for himself. His decision was vetoed authoritatively on the evening of June 20, 1947, when gangland gunners executed Buggsy as he sprawled on a living-room couch in front of a picture window in the Beverly Hills apartment he had set up for Virginia Hill.

The abrupt departure of Buggsy was little more than a minor interlude in the saga of Las Vegas. The mob moguls to whom he had showed the way, and who apparently arranged for his demise, remained. They moved into "The Strip" in massive phalanx, determined to make the desert sprout a lush and perennially rewarding green.

Their presence has been an embarrassment to a state that likes to think it has purified gambling by legalizing it. Actually, legalization has served only to sanctify gangsters who remain their old selves while posing as legitimate businessmen. Time and again since Buggy Siegel's violent removal, the hand of the rackets has shown itself in Nevada, and some of the most famous hotels along the Strip—the Desert Inn, the Thunderbird, the Stardust, and the Tropicana, to cite just a few—have been linked on occasion to the "hidden interests," as Las Vegas calls the underworld.

For years, Virgil Peterson, astute director of the Chicago Crime Commission, has kept a close eye on the flow of syndicate cash into Nevada and the concentration of mob interests there. Repeatedly he has spotted ties that show how virtually every major crime syndicate in the nation has carved itself slices of Nevada's legal gambling pie. In 1950 Peterson reported that Mert Wertheimer and his associates in Detroit were extending their grip on a whole string of hotels and gambling casinos in Reno, Nevada's secondary capital of chance. At the same time close associates of Abner (Longy) Zwillman, the powerful New Jersey rackets boss and collaborator with Adonis and Costello, were dominant figures in a prominent gambling casino in Reno. Jack Dragna, who inherited the California rackets from Buggsy Siegel and earned himself the dread title of "the Capone of Los Angeles," had established another toehold, operating behind fronts in both Reno and Las Vegas.

Occasional legal actions sometimes brought ties like these into the prominence of headlines. In 1950, for example, Texas tried to extradite Lester (Benny) Binnion, long considered the rackets king of Dallas, to face trial on policy charges, but Binnion, ensconced in a legal casino in Las Vegas, successfully defied Texas. Another furor was kicked up in the same year about the activities of Lou Wertheimer, brother of Mert, who was running the gambling concession in a large Reno hotel. Lou Wertheimer's partner was Bernard (Moony) Einstoss, who had once been arrested in California in connection with bribing a jockey. The Reconstruction Finance Corporation had loaned $975,000 in federal funds to the hotel, and some months later Senator William Fulbright and Senator Paul Douglas launched an attack on the ethics of using taxpayers' money to help finance a gambling palace in Reno for Wertheimer-Einstoss interests.

More violent incidents have served from time to time to spotlight mob operations. The Nevada Club, one of the largest downtown gambling casinos in Reno, was operated by Lincoln Fitzgerald and Danny Sullivan. Before coming to Reno, Fitzgerald had been affiliated with Mert Wertheimer in the powerful Michigan syndicate that dominated gambling in Detroit and was linked with the Adonis-Lansky-Costello interests in Florida casinos. Both Fitzgerald and Sullivan had been indicted in Michigan on charges of conspiracy to violate the gambling laws and bribery of police officials, and after a four-year fight had paid fines of $1,000 and court costs of $51,000. This pedigree had been no hindrance to them in Reno, and their Nevada Club proved highly remunerative. Then, about midnight on November 18, 1949, Fitzgerald left his home for the casino. Hidden in the night, a gunman was waiting for him. Two shotgun blasts roared out, and Fitzgerald crumpled to the ground. By some miracle he was not fatally wounded, but Reno shuddered at the prospect of gang wars in its legal paradise. However, for a time at least, nothing else happened.

These early exposures of mob ties were little more than a prelude to a year Nevada can never forget—1954. In this year the entire state was wracked by sensational disclosures showing that mob cash, behind the façade of Nevada's legal casinos, exerted a powerful influence in politics extending to some of the highest echelons in the state. The scandal tumbled out whole closetfuls of skeletons, and in the end decided the governorship.

Nobody had anticipated anything like this in what had been billed as a one-sided gubernatorial contest. The incumbent governor, Charles H. Russell, a Republican, was seeking re-election. His opponent was the popular Vail Pittman. Pittman was a former governor; his brother, the late Key Pittman, had been U.S. Senator; and he had the support of the powerful Democratic machine of Senator Pat McCarran, an irascible and strong-willed figure who for years had dominated Nevada politics. To political observers, it seemed that Russell, despite the advantage that came from holding office, had little chance to win. But then things began to happen.

The first upheaval occurred when members of the Resort Hotel Association of Las Vegas, representing the gambling barons of the Strip, met in private conclave to decide where their cash should go. It was important, of course, that they should have contributions down on the winner, for the gratitude of elected officials is obviously vital to men who need a state license to continue piling up their millions. The hotelmen naturally wanted to make certain that, no matter what the fickle electorate might do, they wouldn't be injured by the outcome. The result was a decision typical in such cases: the gambling moguls agreed to back both sides. But, since Pittman looked like the more certain horse, they would put $60,000 down on him to win; on Russell, they would gamble a mere $15,000.

The details of this bit of statesmanship were supposed, of course, to be confidential; but the very next day the Las Vegas *Sun,* one of the hell-raisingest newspapers in the nation, spread the details all over page one. The plain implication of the *Sun's* story was that, if Pittman were elected, the gamblers would "own" him. This was the first damaging blow struck at Pittman's campaign, but worse was to follow.

To explain what happened next, it is necessary to take a short detour. For years, one of the most famous establishments in the Las Vegas area had been a motel known as Roxie's, located just a few miles out of town. Practically everybody in Las Vegas knew that Roxie's was no ordinary motel. To bed and board, it added broads, regularly housing between twenty and thirty girls, many of them imported from California. The nightly cavalcade that bore well-heeled males from town was hardly a secret to anyone except the law.

Finally, however, someone stepped in to spoil the fun. The interlopers were agents of the FBI. Striking suddenly, they arrested the owners of the fancy brothel, Eddie Clippinger and his wife Roxie, on charges of transporting girls across the California line for immoral purposes. To make the case air-tight, the FBI men raided the motel itself and seized three of its female workers as material witnesses. It was beyond the authority of the FBI to shut up the place, but their action did at least shake up the local law. An hour later Sheriff Glen Jones, who hadn't given any previous indication he was aware that Roxie's even existed, sent a posse and rounded up the rest of the girls.

At this point Herman (Hank) Greenspun, the free-swinging publisher of the Las Vegas *Sun,* jumped into the controversy. In 1,500 acid words, he fired a broadside at the portly, genial Sheriff Jones. "After a brief stakeout of ten years," he wrote, "the sheriff's office amassed sufficient evidence to suspect that Roxie's was not on the list of the Automobile Association of America as one of the approved motels." That was only the beginning. Greenspun charged that the Sheriff had a financial interest in letting Roxie's run. Greenspun accompanied this denunciation with a picture of the Sheriff, a grin spread across his face, astride an old-fashioned bicycle. The caption read: "Sheriff Glen Jones pedaling a little on his own."

In a primary shortly afterwards, the electorate vetoed the Sheriff, who was seeking nomination for his fourth term. Understandably chagrined, the Sheriff sued Greenspun and the *Sun* for $1 million worth of libel. The editor ran the offending editorial and accompanying picture all over again, just, as he said, to show his readers "what a million dollars' worth of prose looks like." But an unanticipated development soon robbed Greenspun of some of his cockiness. He had had a witness, a former employee of Roxie's, who had supplied the details of the motel's secret financial arrangements. Now suddenly this talkative gentleman, summoned before a Clark County grand jury, turned into a clam. Greenspun and the *Sun* were in a spot.

Greenspun, never a man to knuckle under without a fight, went into consultation with his crack crime reporter, Ed Reid. Reid had won a Pulitzer Prize on the old Brooklyn *Eagle* for exposing the $20 million-a-year bookmaking empire of Harry Gross, and he is a man of many resources. He recalled that, during his crime-tracking career in the East, he had come across a fabulous undercover man who went by the improbable name of Pierre LaFitte. Whether the name is real, no one can be certain, but the man who sometimes bears it undeniably is. In the early 1950's, I myself had had reason to admire the skill of LaFitte. At that time, posing as a major racketeer and purchaser of narcotics, he had wormed his way into the confidence of one of the largest narcotics smuggling rings in New York and had helped federal narcotics agents trap some twenty drug importers and peddlers. Ed Reid suggested to Greenspun that he might telephone the undercover wizard and try to persuade him to come west to see what he could do.

One day in early August, 1954, an expensively dressed, stocky man of about 55, speaking with a heavy foreign accent, turned up at El Rancho Vegas, one of the oldest and most expensive establishments on the neon-lighted Strip. The newcomer introduced himself as Louis Tabet and instructed the desk clerk to give him a nice suite well back from the highway because, he said, he and "the missus" wanted rest and privacy. El Rancho is laid out like a miniature village, with guests housed in cottages on private streets winding through landscaped grounds. The desk clerk, eager to oblige the obviously affluent Louis Tabet, installed him in a $30-a-day cottage at 409 Wingy Way, a full three blocks from the Strip. Louis Tabet surveyed the premises and expressed his satisfaction. He promptly called room service and laid in an extensive supply of costly liquor and Corona Coronas. Then he began to wheel and deal.

His first step was to approach the Clippingers with a proposal to buy Roxie's. Despite the unpleasantness with the FBI, the motel had reopened and was doing excellent business. Roxie herself showed Tabet account books indicating that the motel had grossed $77,000 in the past month, a trade that on a yearly basis would figure out to almost $1 million. Under normal circumstances, the Clippingers probably wouldn't have wanted to dispose of such an asset; but, as it was, they had been convicted in federal court on the Mann Act charges, and if they were sent to prison as seemed likely, they could hardly continue to supervise the business. So they were open to a reasonable proposition.

Louis Tabet let it be known that he knew his way around. He had been in the rackets in the East for years, he said, and he understood just how things were done. On his home turf, he confided, "I know just who to grease so the machinery don't squeak," but in Las Vegas he was a stranger and would have to have help to negotiate the right contacts. He was willing to pay, he said, because he always wanted to operate "smooth"; but he wanted to be sure he wasn't paying for nothing. Before Louis Tabet had finished this first conference with Roxie, the madam had recommended to him the services of her brothel manager—a man who, she assured him, knew all the right people—she also advised hiring the legal services of one of the best-known attorneys in the state, Louis Wiener.

This was the opening wedge. Using it, Louis Tabet spent an extremely active six weeks. It wasn't long before some of the most prominent personages in Las Vegas were calling for private consultations in the parlor of Louis Tabet's secluded cottage at 409 Wingy Way. The stocky Tabet made no secret about his underworld background. He was, he assured his callers, a big man in the rackets, and he wanted to invest the bankroll he had amassed in Las Vegas. He was thinking about buying Roxie's but then on the other hand, it might be better to buy into one of the big gambling casinos—there was even more money there. Then, too, if he was going to settle in Las Vegas and operate there permanently, he would have to consider this pestiferous Las Vegas *Sun*. He didn't want trouble, and the *Sun* spelled nothing but trouble. Perhaps he'd have to buy Greenspun out.

As Louis Tabet's multifarious projects expanded, the visitors who called at his Wingy Way cottage became ever more prominent. The official parade began with Sheriff Glen Jones, to whom Tabet unfolded his plans to take over Roxie's. The Sheriff still had several months to serve in office, and Tabet made it clear that, if he bought the place, he would like to make the Sheriff an initial good-will offering of $5,000, to which he would add a steady $1,000 a month. As he said, he always wanted to operate "smooth," and in the meantime, just as a little token of his regard, he'd like the Sheriff to have a $545 television set. The Sheriff sent a truck to cart the set away and was so impressed with the sterling qualities of Louis Tabet that he introduced two Clark County commissioners—powerful members of the local five-man governing board—to the parlor of the big underworld schemer. One of the commissioners departed hugging to his chest a $475 Geiger counter, and assured Louis Tabet, "You've made a commissioner very happy."

Tabet worked up to conferences with attorney Louis Wiener. Now, Wiener was the law partner of Lieutenant Governor Clifford A. Jones (no relation to Sheriff Glen Jones.) The Wiener-Jones law firm represented banks, big corporations, and a long list of Strip resorts and casinos; in addition Cliff Jones held an 11 per cent stock interest in the Thunderbird Hotel. Through Wiener, Louis Tabet arranged an introduction to the Lieutenant Governor. It is worthy of emphasis that no one could have been under any delusions about the background and character of Louis Tabet. In all his conferences, he was brutally frank in describing his racket background, and to all he bragged of his high criminal associations. He confided to Wiener that he was "a good friend" of Dandy Phil Kastel and an equally cordial acquaintance of Jack Dragna, the Al Capone of Los Angeles. This was why, he explained, he couldn't afford to take a blasting from the Las Vegas *Sun*; and why it would be worth it to him to buy the sheet. These frank admissions seemed to place no road blocks in Louis Tabet's way. On the contrary, only three weeks after his arrival in Las Vegas, the self-proclaimed hoodlum went to a private conference with Lieutenant Governor Cliff Jones in the offices of the Thunderbird. Here it was arranged for the number two official in Nevada, together with his law partner, Wiener, to represent Louis Tabet in negotiations for the purchase of the Las Vegas *Sun*.

Wiener now became an even more frequent visitor to Wingy Way. Tabet confided to the attorney that he was worried about the chances of a man with his racket background getting a gaming license from the Nevada Tax Commission. He had heard they could be very stuffy about such pedigrees. Wiener advised that it might be the part of wisdom to hold up on his investments until after the election. Once Pittman was elected Governor, the attorney assured Tabet, there would be changes in the tax commission. "Cliff," Wiener said, speaking of his law partner, would then be "the number one guy in the state."

Louis Tabet found occasion to inject into the conversation a remark about the Thunderbird and Lieutenant Governor Jones' financial interest in it. "I know that Jake Lansky, Meyer Lansky, everybody's in it," Tabet remarked to Wiener, and said that he had discussed "Meyer and Jake" and the Thunderbird with Lieutenant Governor Jones in their private conference in the hotel's office. The unsuspecting Wiener agreed that "Meyer and Jake are in the Thunderbird."

Then Louis Tabet suddenly lost interest in all the grandiose business ventures he had discussed with the politicians of Las Vegas. He simply paid his $3,900 bill at El Rancho Vegas, packed his bags and departed.

Before his newly cultivated friends had a chance to notice his disappearance, they were given the reason for it in boxcar type across page one of the Las Vegas *Sun*. Ed Reid began to tell all in twelve articles exposing the intimate talks that had been held with hoodlum Louis Tabet in the parlor of 409 Wingy Way, while tape recorders ran quietly in a convenient closet.

For Louis Tabet, of course, had been none other than Pierre LaFitte, the undercover agent imported by the *Sun*. He had found the politicians of Las Vegas not half so hard to deal with as the narcotics mobs he had duped back in the East. The first thing Louis Tabet had done when he established himself in El Rancho was to wire his room for sound; and in the latter stages of his enterprise, after he began to get chummy with important personages, he had two eyewitnesses to every conversation—reporter Ed Reid and Gordon Hawkins, assistant to the District Attorney of Clark County, both hidden with the tape recorders in the capacious closet.

The reverberations of the *Sun*'s day-by-day exposés shook the entire state of Nevada. In rapid succession came these developments:

The Clark County grand jury indicted Sheriff Jones and the Clark County commissioner who had been so happy with his Geiger counter, charging them with accepting gifts and offers of money in return for agreeing to use their official positions to further the schemes of the self-proclaimed hoodlum, Louis Tabet.

The State's Democratic leaders hastily convened and just as hastily accepted the resignation of Lieutenant Governor Jones as Democratic National Committeeman, a post of honor to which he had only recently been elevated.

Sheriff Jones dropped his $1 million libel suit against the *Sun.*

And the voters of the state went to the polls and turned thumbs down on the gubernatorial candidacy of Vail Pittman, re-electing Governor Russell—an unexpected result that was attributed almost solely to the impact made upon the public by the Las Vegas scandal.

In addition to all this, the Nevada Tax Commission started proceedings against the Thunderbird, charging that under existing management it was unfit to hold a gaming license. A key element in the tax commission's case involved the charge that the Lieutenant Governor of Nevada had been a business partner of the notorious Meyer and Jake Lansky. In testimony before the commission, Cliff Jones emphatically denied that the Lanskys had a piece of the Thunderbird. When told the commission had a tape recording of his conversation with Louis Tabet, the Lieutenant Governor challenged the commissioners to produce it, and when they declined for the moment, he refused to answer any more questions.

Louis Wiener, the Lieutenant Governor's law partner, was an equally unhappy witness. He admitted he had made the prediction that, if Pittman were elected, he would change the personnel of the tax commission. Wiener wasn't quite so specific, however, concerning his conversation with

Tabet about the Lanskys' interest in the Thunderbird. He insisted he had "no independent recollection" of making the statement, but conceded: "If you have a tape recording of my voice at the El Rancho, I presume I said what it says."

But in the end, as is usually the case, nothing much happened. The indictments against the former Sheriff and the Clark County Commissioner hung fire for a couple of years; but then, since Louis Tabet had not, after all, set up any illegal business or received any actual protection, the charges were quashed. The case against the Thunderbird was for a time more serious. The Nevada tax commission produced evidence that seemed conclusive—the federal income tax returns of George Sadlo, a major Lansky henchman and bodyguard, and Jake Lansky himself. These documents showed the pair had paid taxes on $200,000 worth of income from the Thunderbird. The Nevada commission revoked the hotel's gaming license, but the verdict was fought into the State Supreme Court, where the Thunderbird obtained a reversal of the commission's decision and regained its license.

With time the scandal faded and died, but in Nevada the memory of it lingers on. Only a highly unusual series of coincidences—the raid on Roxie's, Greenspun's libel involvement with Sheriff Jones, a heated gubernatorial contest, all occurring at the same time—had lifted the lid on what goes on secretly at America's gaudiest gambling Mecca. It was a glimpse that exposed the ties forged by underworld billions—the partnership mobster money has purchased with businessmen and politicians. The moral of the lesson is plain, and it holds true far beyond the boundaries of Las Vegas and Nevada. When money in limitless amounts speaks with so loud a voice, its possessors become respectable. It is a formula that unites the interests of brothel keepers and mobsters with those of lawyers and businessmen, law enforcement officers and politicians, in a chain of influence that stretches all too frequently from the lowest to the highest levels.

This admittedly is not a pretty vision, and Nevada was so much disturbed by it that, beginning in 1955, it attempted to impose more stringent regulations on the kind of gentlemen it permitted to bankroll its pure games of chance. Prior to this time, Nevada had made little more than token efforts to keep out the mob. True, it did screen applicants for licenses to run its gambling parlors, and though its tax commission could be tough on occasion, the screens that were generally used were decidedly large-mesh. For example, peccadillos like bootlegging convictions and gambling convictions in a man's past did not count. Nevada didn't consider these real crimes. Officials explained that, since Nevada considered gambling a legitimate enterprise, it could hardly discriminate against individuals who might have compiled police records yards long by plying this trade in less enlightened states. The result was that some of the nastiest and most powerful figures in the American underworld found in Nevada an ideal legal haven for the investment of their racket millions, just so long as they had the good sense to keep themselves a few steps removed from any direct connection with such offenses as narcotics peddling, and murder, crimes on which even Nevada frowned.

In 1955 the Nevada Gaming Control Board was set up, with a former FBI expert to run its staff, and greater emphasis was placed on keeping out the mob. This was an attempt, however, that met with only indifferent success, as was demonstrated two years later with the discovery of the Tropicana gambling report in the pocket of the wounded Frank Costello. Even later, in 1959, when Lester Velie probed Las Vegas for a scathing report in the *Reader's Digest,* he found "the hidden interests" still wielding heavy influence along the Strip.

Velie focused an especially strong spotlight on the Desert Inn, probably the most famous of the Strip's gambling palaces. Run ostensibly by a flamboyant showman and greeter named Wilbur Clark, the place became known as Wilbur Clark's Desert Inn; but for years, from its founding in 1950 down to a shift in stock ownership in late 1959, it was really the mob's. "The lists of licenses . . . read like a page out of a U.S. Senate investigation of the Cleveland underworld," Velie wrote. Identical shares totaling 40 per cent of the stock were held by Moe Dalitz, one-time bootlegger and gambling figure in Cleveland; his partner, Maurice Kleinman, who had served a three-year term for income-tax evasion; and Sam Tucker, another ex-bootlegger and gambler. The same combine had also moved in and acquired 66 per cent of the stock of the Stardust Hotel and casino, advertised as "the world's largest resort hotel." The Stardust had been founded by Tony Stralla, a Los Angeles gangster, and its casino manager (and holder of 5 per cent stock interest) was none other than John Drew, long denounced by Virgil Peterson in Chicago as the right-hand man of Tony Accardo.

Such ties are enough to raise serious questions about what really goes on behind the ceaselessly clanking slots and whirring wheels of Las Vegas. This incredible gambling city stuns every newspaperman who visits it for the first time. It has become stereotype to begin an impressionistic journalistic piece with a line like: "I've just seen Las Vegas, but I still can't believe it." In Las Vegas there is no such thing as time. The gambling casinos roar at frenetic tempo around the clock, 24 hours a day, without pause or letup. Three shifts of employees work the gambling tables. The money never stops flowing; it is routine to see a big plunger drop $75,000 at a crap table in a few hours. Stories are commonplace about the player on a lucky streak who piled up a fortune, kept gambling for more, lost all—and had to borrow money to get out of town. Most Las Vegas stories end up with that last line: "He had to borrow money to get out of town."

No one who knows the American underworld, its ruthlessness and insatiable greed, can remain long under the delusion that it runs this fabulous gold mine with ministerial rectitude. Only one thing is probably true about the Las Vegas operation: the games themselves are honest —that is, crooked dice, rigged roulette wheels, gimmicked slot machines are frowned upon. Las Vegas wants the visiting sucker to retain the silly idea that he has a chance, and so it's content to take the normal house percentages, knowing that these, operating 24 hours a day, are certain to separate any visitor from his wealth. This noble restraint has led to the widely purveyed myth that Las Vegas is pure down to the tips of its toes, an unlikely eventuality with so many hardened racketeers pulling strings behind the scenes.

Much more worthy of belief are persistent reports from responsible sources who maintain that one of Las Vegas' greatest appeals lies in the opportunity it offers to finagle with the internal revenue laws. Knowledgeable persons in Hollywood insist that one of Las Vegas' most persuasive allures is to be found in the possibility its gambling offers for tax-free income. The fantastic prices paid by hotels along the Strip for the best Hollywood and

New York entertainment talent have been widely ballyhooed. Yet actually, according to Hollywood sources, headline entertainers are sometimes willing to play Las Vegas for considerably less than they might otherwise demand and get because they are being slipped "under the table" a bundle of cash, ostensibly "gambling winnings"—extra money that is extremely difficult for Internal Revenue to trace.

There are many variations on this theme. It is obvious that Las Vegas plays an important role in legitimatizing mob money. A racketeer who buys himself a healthy share of one of the huge casinos has acquired a legitimate source of heavy income; and if he reports and pays taxes on $200,000, as the Lansky Brothers did in the Thunderbird, he has established such a huge base of legal and reported wealth that it becomes extremely difficult for tax men to attack his accounts by establishing his net worth—that is, showing he spent more than he reported. Even if a racketeer has an extra $100,000 in cash at his disposal, the task of tracking and showing this, when he has acknowledged so much, becomes infinitely complicated if not impossible.

The gaming tables themselves occasionally serve a similar function. If, as sometimes happens, a shady character with more money that is good for him hits a short lucky streak and wins a $50,000 potful in the presence of scores of witnesses, he has publicly established a reportable source of heavy money and can attribute a bountiful supply of cash to gambling winnings. He may lose it back the next day (and certainly will if he keeps on playing), but the reportable winnings enable him to account for the kind of spending money he might otherwise find it hard to explain.

Finally, and most importantly, the torrent of cash that flows through the gambling halls of Nevada runs largely without official check or control. The accounts of the gambling casinos are a law unto themselves. The figures they report become official figures, and there is virtually no way of determining whether they report all, much, or little. One of the most persistent reports in Nevada—one that, for instance, is believed by Internal Revenue men—insists that there is an "off the top" racket annually siphoning off huge sums before official casino tallies are compiled and presented to the state for tax purposes.

This aspect of Las Vegas struck John Gunther most forcibly a few years ago when he did one of his "inside" probes of this gambling madhouse. "One striking point is that no really accurate inspection of the cash take, on which the most important tax depends, is possible," Gunther wrote. "The big casinos run 24 hours a day, in three shifts, without interruption, and the money is hauled off and counted after each shift. . . . Obviously, the state cannot afford to have inspectors to watch the counting in each casino—a dramatic moment—at the end of every shift. It would take hundreds of men. So the casinos furnish affidavits as to the amount of the take, three times a day, and these have to be signed by at least two witnesses. Even so, a bit of cash probably leaks away."

Internal Revenue men suspect that it is quite a bit. With only a handful of agents in Las Vegas, Internal Revenue is even more handicapped than the state in checking up on the flood from the gaming tables. This leaves the casinos as the final authority on their own reapings. Their reports show that they compile a gross profit of about $200 million a year, with roughly 20 per cent coming from slot machines. While $200 million is a lot of money, it does not seem to be an extravagant haul when one considers that an estimated seven million tourists annually plunge some $3 billion into the capacious maws of Nevada's one-armed bandits and the greedy "drop-boxes" under the card, dice, and roulette tables.

The casino's accounting system is a masterpiece of simplicity and secrecy. When a customer hands a "box man" at a dice table $10 to buy chips or silver dollars, the "box man" drops the ten-spot through a slot in the table into a locked "drop-box" beneath. Into this box also go receipts known as "fill slips" which indicate how much money has been brought to the table from the house's cashier cage during a working shift. At the end of the shift, the "drop-box" is taken, still locked, from the gaming table to the counting room. There it is unlocked and its contents tallied. By subtracting the "fill slips" from the cash total, the house's gross win from that particular table is obtained. This system of locked "drop-boxes" and sequestered accounting is obviously ideal for finagling; when no spot check is being made by the state and the winnings are heavy, it obviously would be simple to whack substantial amounts "off the top" before the final figures were compiled.

There is just one factor that inhibits the full-blown operation of such a delightful racket. Where gangster ownership is widely spread and important mob stockholders reside in distant states, the count almost has to be honest, not so much for the state's sake as for internal harmony. Since no racketeer ever climbed to high estate by trusting his fellows, it follows that each absentee landlord would want assurance from some trusted hand that he wasn't being gypped. This, indeed, was one significant aspect of the private report on the Tropicana's earnings found in Frank Costello's pocket; Costello evidently felt that such a secret memo, confirming the officially reported Tropicana figures, was essential for his fiscal welfare.

It does not follow, however, that all Las Vegas casino figures are so scrupulously exact. In casinos more tightly controlled, with the principal partners on the scene, the opportunity exists to extract considerable quantities of boodle. From time to time, Las Vegas has been shaken by reports—and occasional scattered testimony—indicating that such a racket exists on a handsome scale. Lester Velie cited some of the more notable examples in his *Reader's Digest* article.

"One big casino operator is reported to take $10,000 off the top daily," Velie wrote. "This is a fantastic figure—it would come to more than $3 million yearly—but Las Vegas is a fantastic place.

"A method of knocking money off the top at counting time was described by a casino auditor who got into a hassle with his employers. The auditor testified in a bankruptcy proceeding that the former owners of a casino knocked so much off the top that the gambling place paid no taxes for the five years he was employed there. A former cashier in the place, now in the Internal Revenue Service, stated in a deposition in a lawsuit that when money from the gaming tables was counted, substantial sums were taken out and put in envelopes in the casino's vault. Weekly, there would arrive from Los Angeles a brother-in-law of one of the casino owners. He would come in at night, pick up the envelopes, and make for Los Angeles."

No one knows how prevalent such "off-the-top" looting is or how much money it represents. Governor Grant Sawyer of Nevada insists that "an expert staff of auditors and investigators, empowered by law to be in on the 'first count' of any casino at any time, haven't been able to find evidence in support of such rumors." But he admitted in an interview with Velie that he was painfully aware there were "hidden interests" in the casinos and that he also suspected "there is probably considerable unaccounted-for vagrant cash going somewhere," depriving both the state and federal governments "of unknown amounts of taxes."

Whatever the full truth about the hidden rackets of Las Vegas, it seems indisputable that Nevada's experiment with legalized gambling hasn't been the happy and unqualified success that has been usually pictured. What Nevada has done is to provide a legal refuge for some of the most ruthless mobsters in America. It has made "fun-loving" Las Vegas a city of pivotal influence in American crime.

The control that is exercised from Las Vegas, the ties that link the capital of legal gambling with illegal activities throughout the rest of the United States, have been exposed in many ways. Let's look at a few examples.

In the fall of 1957, federal agents raided a huge syndicate "layoff" headquarters that had set up shop in Terre Haute, Indiana. A federal grand jury sitting in Indianapolis subsequently heard testimony from 170 persons coming from forty states—graphic evidence of the tentacles that stretched out from Terre Haute and covered most of the nation. Federal accountants determined that in three months of operations the "layoff" headquarters had accepted $3,363,152 in bets. Eight top operators were subsequently indicted and convicted. It was hardly by chance, in an operation so huge, that they divided neatly into groups that demonstrated the amalgamation of mob interests. Two were representatives of the Chicago mob, one was from Detroit, three were local Indiana contacts, and the last two were from Las Vegas.

Federal investigations time and again have pinpointed Las Vegas as a center of important mob influence. The

New York City policy investigation indicated that the real masterminds of the racket pull directional wires from remote headquarters in Miami and Nevada. As Joseph Manners told the New York State investigation, the checkup phone calls to Biloxi and Covington to see how "layoff" business is doing come from Las Vegas, a clear indication that top-level mob control is centered there.

The same fact was demonstrated by one of the early discoveries by Milton Wessel's rackets-busting team. A group of its agents in Florida stopped a courier who was returning from a Caribbean jaunt with an innocent-looking suitcase. The courier was none other than Jake Lansky, and the suitcase, on examination, turned out to be not so innocent. It was, in fact, as crammed as Buggsy Siegel's two satchels during the building of the Flamingo. It contained $200,000 in cash, the profits of syndicate gambling ventures in Havana, and an additional $50,000 worth of checks. Though there was no way of determining the intended destination of Lansky's cash, there could be no doubt about the checks. They had all been made out to a Florida agent who represented Las Vegas interests.

Such are the ties that thread from Las Vegas across the nation. They suggest that the entire country is paying a heavy price for Nevada's fling with legalized gambling. But whatever the national price may be, the price to Nevada itself is far heavier. The publicity mills of Las Vegas churn out puffs about the stage shows, the high-priced entertainers, the romances and gaudy trappings of the Strip. But there is no publicity mill to deal with another and more important story—the story of the misery, destitution, and despair that are the inevitable legacy of unrestricted gambling. It isn't considered polite to point out that, in Nevada, the pawnshops do just as frantic a business as the gambling casinos.

The stories of the tourists who have been lured to have their fling in this gay and exciting capital of chance —and have become so broke and desperate they can find neither the means nor the courage to leave—are legion. It is commonplace to see a man walk into a pawnshop—his money, jewelry, wrist watch already gone—and ask the proprietor: "What will you give me for these glasses?" As he holds his eyeglasses in his hand, he is gently informed that Nevada regulations prevent hock shops from loaning money on devices essential to health such as glasses, hearing aids, and false teeth. This is virtually the only limit on the plucking.

Typical of the individual tragedies that Nevada breeds is the story of a young couple who had come West on their honeymoon. Both had worked before their marriage, and they had saved up a sizeable bankroll. It occurred to them that it would be fun to take a little fling to see if they could increase their stake in Reno. What happened, of course, is what usually happens. The young bridegroom began to lose and couldn't stop. The more he lost, the more desperately he tried to "get even." All their money gone, the young husband sold their car—and gambled away the proceeds. His bride got a job as a waitress to support them, but not even the shame of dependency upon her earnings could jolt the bridegroom back to reason. He hocked everything they had, their clothes, their luggage—and gambled away every last cent.

"Finally," said the social-service expert who recalled this story, "they were evicted from a rooming house and slept two nights in a bus station. Not until then did the girl swallow her pride and wire her parents in Oklahoma for help."

In Nevada, this is not considered an unusual story; such examples of heart-break are so common that they hardly rate as news any more. As Ed Reid, the Las Vegas reporter, says bitterly about gambling: "We're stuck with this thing. It doesn't take a moralist to see that this is all wrong. The temptations are too much for almost anyone. I've seen church bishops playing the slots. Our local Catholic Charities allocates almost its entire budget to getting stranded people out of town—getting them gasoline, food baskets, and cash."

Inevitably, in such an atmosphere, crime rates soar. Both Las Vegas and Reno maintain exceptionally large and costly police departments for cities of their size, attesting to the difficulty of maintaining order in a gambling society, in a climate of easy virtue in which all distinctions become blurred. It is perhaps no coincidence that Reno had a major police scandal in 1960. Seven police officers were suspended, and six signed confessions, admitting that they had been active in a burglary ring responsible for looting ten business establishments. Crimes that spring from monetary desperation—robberies and burglaries—are far more numerous in Las Vegas and Reno than they are in much larger cities in other states. And the Nevada suicide rate is frequently double the average for the rest of the nation.

A few statistics taken from the FBI's Uniform Crime Report for 1959, the bible on the incidence of crime across the nation, illustrate the disproportionate records of Nevada's twin gambling cities. Las Vegas, with a population of 63,453, reported 86 robberies and 788 burglaries in 1959. Reno, with 50,938 residents, outstripped Las Vegas in robberies with 93 and had an almost equally high burglary figure, 676. The significance of such statistics becomes apparent when one places them side by side with the records of a couple of California cities of comparable size—Santa Barbara, with 58,259 residents, and Santa Clara, with

58,577. Santa Barbara reported just 12 robberies and 408 burglaries; Santa Clara, 16 robberies and 172 burglaries. Such a comparison is not unfair to the Nevada cities. In crime statistics, it is not hard to find cities twice the size of Reno and Las Vegas with half the crime. Lincoln, Nebraska, is an example. It has a population of 127,433, slightly more than double that of Las Vegas. Yet in 1959 it had only 11 robberies to Las Vegas' 86; only 328 burglaries, compared to Las Vegas' 788.

Under the circumstances it is hardly surprising that the crime rate for the entire state of Nevada is the highest of any state in the nation. The FBI compilation on seven categories of major crimes gives Nevada the unenviable number one spot, with an incidence of 1,915.8 crimes for each 100,000 population. Among its immediate neighbors, only California, a much larger and more populous state, comes anywhere near close, with a rate of 1,635.8 crimes per 100,000. Nevada's other neighbors rank like this: Arizona, 1,500.2 crime per 100,000; Utah, 827.1; Oregon, 819.4; and Idaho, 657.6.

Such crime rates mock the industriously purveyed myth of Nevada's "success" with legal gambling. They tell a grimmer story, one that should make any other state think twice before it tries to emulate Nevada and let down the bars on gambling.

Yet, in Nevada, such facts are not so much blandly denied as blandly ignored. Officials continue to brag about their "success" in controlling gambling and maintaining an upright and law-abiding society. One of their favorite boasts is that Nevada has not been blitzed with mob wars and gangland executions. This, like most of Nevada's pretensions, is at best only partly true. It is not especially surprising to find that the underworld has refrained from sullying its legal nest in Nevada with mass mayhem; after all, the top brains of the underworld are no morons, and even a moron would recognize that gang guns might turn the lovely legal oasis in Nevada right back to arid desert. But this does not mean that the muscle of the mob, its will to murder, is entirely absent from the operations in Las Vegas.

After all, Buggsy Siegel did not die an exactly natural death. He did not become a homicide statistic in Las Vegas; that was an honor reserved for the state of California. Similarly, in the more recent past, history seems to have repeated itself in the fate that overtook one of Buggsy's successors.

When Buggsy was erased by carbine fire while sprawling on Virginia Hill's couch, it became necessary for someone to take over the management of his gaudy Flamingo. This honor fell to one of Buggsy's close associates, Gus Greenbaum, a former bookie. There wasn't much secret about whose interests Greenbaum was protecting, and for years he protected well. But then he moved from the Flamingo to the new Riviera Hotel, and there, just like Buggsy, he began to get grandiose ideas. He wanted to enlarge the Riviera by lavishing an additional $2 million upon it. There was opposition to this, and in December, 1959, Gus Greenbaum and his wife were found trussed up, their throats slashed, in their home in Phoenix, Arizona. As far as Las Vegas was concerned, this was strictly Arizona's problem; but Nevada cannot escape at least the basic moral responsibility for some of the gory trade practices that happen elsewhere.

8

SHALL GOVERNMENT JOIN THE BOOKIES?

"ANY society that bases its financial structure on the weaknesses of its people doesn't deserve to survive."

This was the comment of Police Chief William Parker of Los Angeles on New York City's proposal to legalize bookmaking. In this one blunt sentence is expressed the essence of the whole issue of gambling as a major means of revenue to support the structure of modern government.

Discussing New York's proposal to extend the sanction of the law from the track to the bookie parlor, Chief Parker argued that the legalization of off-track betting would attract additional underworld elements and would lead to more vice and corruption. He mentioned also that the legalization of bookmaking would serve only to increase temptation for weak characters, some of whom might even plead as an excuse that they were patriotically helping to defray the costs of government!

By contrast, many of our official spokesmen today argue that a little further legalization of the gambling rackets, especially of bookmaking, won't hurt anybody; it is inevitable, they say, and, besides, it will solve beautifully all taxation problems. The mayors of New York for the past ten years have persisted in this viewpoint. Former Mayor William O'Dwyer first suggested legalization of bookmaking, and Mayor Wagner's $2-billion-a-year city administration continued to hug the proposal to its breast, advocating it with ever greater ardor.

The present Wagner administration by its own estimates has pleaded guilty to the sin of permitting a $5-billion-a-year illegal bookmaking operation to flourish right under the nose of the largest police department in the nation. It has pleaded in effect that it is helpless to curb this lawlessness, and that the only thing that can be done is to yield to human "instinct," join the bookies, and get the revenue. In its proposal to the State Legislature in 1960, it suggested that if off-track bookmaking were legalized a credit system should be installed so that even gambling addicts who didn't have cash in pocket at the moment could be encouraged to bet against their futures. Such proposals touch off a great annual debate, much of it conducted in a vacuum. It is a war of clichés in which little attention is paid to past experience.

Clearly, such an issue cannot be understood without a little historical perspective. What has been America's experience with legalized gambling? Where has it been tried? How has it worked? Las Vegas is usually cited by proponents of legalization as the realization of the millennium, but this is clearly an idealized portrait. Besides, Las Vegas is not the only criterion. America's experience with legalized gambling stretches back over hundreds of years and falls into a pattern. Waves of addiction have resulted in such excesses that waves of reform have followed. The strict anti-gambling laws of most states are not, as the propaganda of the gambling interests would have us believe, the product of puritanical prudery, but rather the result of disastrous prior experience.

The most significant pattern emerges from a study of America's oldest and most popular form of gambling—the lottery. Lotteries flourished from earliest colonial days. In fact, the Virginia Colony when it was first established was financed largely by the proceeds of lotteries run in London by the Virginia Company under a grant from the Crown. The first lottery was highly successful; its successors far less so. Before long, tradesmen were complaining that gambling fever had demoralized business and industry. Abuses grew. One of the managers was accused of embezzling 7,000 to 8,000 pounds and then bribing an auditor to conceal his theft. In the end, the lottery franchise was repealed.

Throughout the colonial period, lotteries were a favorite means of raising revenue for worth-while projects—to build bridges, roads, town halls, schools. Early universities—Harvard, Yale and Columbia, to name just three—were financed in their first years partly by the proceeds from lotteries. But the lure of cheap money, of "something for nothing," was then, as now, deeply corrupting. Rackets began to flourish. Lottery tickets were counterfeited and sold by the thousands to a deceived public; professional operators wormed their way into the management of legal lotteries and filched their funds; business interests protested that the gambling fever siphoned away money that should be spent by the people for their legitimate needs—that, in a word, gambling injured all trade.

Following the Revolution, many states discovered that only greedy professional promoters seemed to be deriving any real benefit from the lotteries. In 1819 the New York Legislature conducted a probe and found defalcations in three lottery offices amounting to $109,144.99. The investigating committee maintained that "the system is so radically vicious" that it could not be controlled by legislation. A Pennsylvania committee discovered similar abuses, came to the same conclusion, and urged that "this blot" be wiped away and lotteries never again be used in Pennsylvania as a method of finance. By 1833 virtually all lotteries throughout the United States had been abolished.

The post-Civil War era saw a revival of the lottery. Several states, especially in the war-racked South, legalized lotteries as a means of raising revenue. Once more the cycle of abuse, scandal, corruption, and belated reform began. Louisiana became the most glaring example of the vices of legal gambling. The Louisiana Lottery Company was given a charter in 1869 to run for twenty-five years. The company was exempt from taxation. It operated under a façade of charity, pledged to contribute $40,000 annually to the New Orleans Charity Hospital. Its history and the tremendous evil influence it exerted in Louisiana were thus described by Virgil Peterson in testimony before a committee of the Canadian Parliament in 1955:

"The Louisiana Lottery Company soon learned that although officials of the state government might be ignorant, they were highly expensive. Legislators not only had to be bought, it was necessary to make them stay bought. According to affidavits executed by two of the incorporators, at least $300,000 was paid in bribes by the lottery company during the first seven years of its existence. . . . It is well known that for about twenty years it virtually controlled Louisiana politically. Governors, United States Senators, judges owed their positions to the influence of the lottery company. . . . In the state election of 1892, the lottery served as the sole issue in the contest for governor. Louisiana—perhaps less than other states—could not be charged as being a center of puritanism, but the people, knowing the bad experience they had, went to the polls and outlawed the lottery."

What such experience seems to indicate is simply this: that all betting is bad and corruptive, that the flood of cheap money big-time gambling lures corrodes both the morals of the betting public and the morals of officials charged with its supervision. The question arises not just about the extension of legalization, but about the legalization of pari-mutuels that has already taken place, and about the dependence of state governments upon the millions of dollars of revenue derived from them. If large-scale, commercial betting by its very nature corrupts, it is obvious that even pari-mutuels represent a weakening of the fiber of democratic society. This is a view that is hardly ever expressed; pari-mutuels are accepted as an established fact of modern life, and the ethical question of whether their influence has been good or evil is one that is not even considered. But perhaps it should be, for there is considerable evidence to indicate that the legalization of pari-mutuels represented a greater boon to the mob than Prohibition.

The legalization of on-track betting through the installation of the pari-mutuel system came in most states in the depression-ridden thirties. It represented, in effect, the reversal of decisions taken by prior generations disgusted with the excesses of gambling. But the new system was sold to the public on the basis of its mechanical purity, on the grounds that it would eliminate the bookmakers who infested many tracks, and with the promise that it would produce easy revenue for the financially hard-pressed states. Pari-mutuels were pictured as a mechanical antidote to the rackets; a comparison was drawn between the puritanical strictures imposed by the highly unpopular Prohibition law and the strictures on gambling; and in the wave of revulsion against the folly of liquor legislation, and in the financial crisis of the times, state after state yielded to the arguments of the racing interests, and the great wave of modern gambling was born.

It has not been sufficiently realized what a boon this was to the mob. Prohibition, which had poured millions into the treasuries of gangdom—Prohibition, which had given the cheapest thugs of the underworld millionaire status and had enabled them to organize crime on a syndicate basis—was expiring. With its death, the underworld desperately needed a replacement racket; and it was gangdom's good fortune that, just at this delicate moment, the states began to legalize pari-mutuels. What happened was inevitable—and yet unexpected. Betting at the tracks fostered betting off the tracks, and gambling mushroomed quickly into a multi-billion-dollar business, far more remunerative to the underworld than Prohibition had ever been.

The Massachusetts Crime Commission summarized this development in these words:

"There has doubtless been in this country from time immemorial professional activity in the taking and making of bets on horse races. The true bookmaker or gambler on horse racing is to be found throughout our literature. But the rise of this activity to the status of business is recent. It is significant that the Massachusetts Commission of 1933 gave it no attention. The operation of licensed pari-mutuel tracks in this area began in 1935. The Commission dates from that time the beginning and growth in Massachusetts of the huge business under consideration. This business, here and throughout the country, is based, as this report will show, on opportunity provided by publicly accepted pari-mutuel racing. It is of interest that the golden stream from unlawful liquor supply cut off by Prohibition repeal in 1933 was shortly replaced by a stream rising from the legalized pari-mutuel source. Legislatures in licensing honest, pari-mutuel betting doubtless did not contemplate that, as professionals have told the Commission as an axiom, every one who bets at the track will, given the chance, bet away from the track. . . .

"Bookies interviewed by the Commission have represented all levels in the business. They have had no disposition to be helpful, but they have made some helpful disclosures. As above stated, it is their rule of thumb that he who will bet at the track will bet away from the track. All agree that the business is a year-round business, but it is better when the New England tracks are operating than when the play is based only on tracks in California, Florida, Maryland, or elsewhere. They agree that the local season (235 calendar days in 1955, with, due to overlapping schedules, 278 racing days at licensed pari-mutuel horse tracks) is a continuous period of good business. They agree that the amount bet on horses away from licensed tracks is far bigger than that bet at the windows. . . ."

The New York Commission of Investigation, in its cross-state bookmaking probe, duplicated the discoveries of the Massachusetts commission. It found that bookmaking activity rose sharply when New York tracks were open; it found that the betting tempo picked up in the immediate area around a local track and that, in sections of the state far removed from any track, betting on sports tended to be heavier. "All of this is logical," Bill Walsh points out. "When a track is open nearby, it stimulates interest, and then, in addition, you have all the usual flood of hot tips and rumors that promote action."

Such findings clearly indicate the close relationship between legal pari-mutuel betting and the illegal bookmaking that bankrolls the underworld. It is almost startling to discover that the Massachusetts Crime Commission found that bookmaking, the most important racket of the underworld today, did not even rate as a crime problem worthy of mention in 1933, two years before pari-mutuels were legalized. It is significant that both the Massachusetts and New York commissions discovered a close relationship between local racing and bookmaking activity. This helps explain the tremendous growth of bookmaking across the nation, since pari-mutuels have led to the founding of many new tracks, opening up betting activity in areas where it previously had not existed.

These developments have in turn increased the pressures for off-track legalization. It is argued that we embrace a hypocritical double standard of morality when we sanction betting at the track, but outlaw it away from the track. "There always has and always will be gambling, and it is no more wrong to bet outside the track than inside the fence," we are often told. But, as the Massachusetts commission pointed out, there are fundamental differences between the two operations. Race track owners do at least furnish large and costly plants for the enjoyment of their patrons; they maintain payrolls, keep horses in hay, provide a service that offers valid entertainment. There is undeniable enjoyment in participating in the excitement and drama of a stirring horse race run in the open air in fine surroundings; aside from betting, there is real recreational value. By contrast, the bookie provides nothing; he is a parasite feeding on the weakness of others, furnishing no useful service to anyone, satisfying nothing but his own greed. Equally parasitical is the bettor who patronizes him. All the bettor is seeking is a fast killing—the pot of gold at the end of the rainbow that shall be his with no effort, no expenditure of labor or talent. The bettor and bookie, in their separate ways, deserve each other, and each expresses for the other, as the Massachusetts commission noted, nothing but complete contempt. Such are the lovely foundations on which the underworld has built an entire way of life. Such are the basic differences between on-track and off-track betting. Recognition of the valid elements of one, the unmitigated evil of the other, is vital. As the Massachusetts commission said bluntly, "There has not always been gambling with organized racketeers on a scale which amounts to a state of lawlessness in an entire society, and there need not be."

The intrinsic evil of gambling for gambling's sake, even under legal auspices, has been demonstrated in virtually every state in which it has ever been tried. New Mexico and Arizona, in the days before they were admitted to the Union as states in 1907, permitted gambling to operate legally upon the payment of license fees. Between 700 and 1,000 gambling dens opened in the two territories. Tough crowds of miners, cowboys, Chinese, and Mexicans crowded the streets and jammed the gaming tables. Subsequent investigations showed that most of the houses resorted to outrageous cheating. Herbert J. Hagerman, Governor of New Mexico in 1906 and 1907, said in a message to the Territorial Council that some of the games offered a player 250 per cent less chance of winning than similar games in European casinos that always returned fortunes to their stockholders. Fleeced customers frequently became irate and shot up the joints that had parted them from their money. Both territories after they became states passed anti-gambling laws.

In more recent times, both Idaho and Montana, beguiled perhaps by reports of Nevada's happy experience with legal gambling, decided to try the experiment. In

1947 Idaho passed a law which permitted municipalities to license slot machines on a local option basis. Many took advantage of the opportunity. The city of Twin Falls licensed slot machines and took 50 per cent of the gross proceeds after allowing the operators 10 per cent for maintenance. The city obtained revenue, but soon found itself involved in a noisome mire. The police commissioner discovered that an underworld syndicate controlled many of the licensed machines. A patrolman was convicted of obtaining $1,000 from a café owner to insure the continuance of his slot-machine license. The relief rolls grew because people of little income poured their all into the slots and became destitute. Armed robberies increased. With evils multiplying on every hand, the city council of Twin Falls in January, 1949, canceled all slot-machine licenses. The cities of Boise, Nampa, and Rupert had similar experiences and took similar action. The Idaho Municipal League denounced the partnership of government with slot machine interests, and Idaho abandoned legalized gambling.

Montana had a parallel adventure. It legalized punch boards and enacted a statute permitting the maintenance of slot machines in private clubs. In 1947 alone, 179 so-called private clubs were incorporated, and by 1949 more than 600 studded the state. Many of these were mere fronts for slot-machine interests, and their "private" status was discounted by prominently displayed signs that read: "Public Invited." Legitimate business suffered, relief rolls lengthened, abuses grew. As early as 1947 Governor Sam C. Ford commented that "the condition of the state is worse than it has been for many years in reference to gambling," and in a special address in November, he conceded frankly that his "two outstanding mistakes were when I signed the slot machine law and the punch board law." Montana, like Idaho, soon abandoned its disastrous experiment with legal gambling.

Everywhere one turns, gambling seems to have smirched all it touches. America's historical experience has been that hardly any large lottery, no matter how ethically it begins, continues in the long run to be conducted with probity; that every oasis of legal gambling inevitably tends to become fouled in a mire of rackets, destitution, and corruption. Only one major lottery that has flourished for years seems to have remained an exception to the rule and to have retained, in the popular mind at least, an image of unsullied purity. This is the Irish Sweepstakes.

The Sweeps, run off three times a year and based on the winner of horse races held in England, are a favorite gamble for all classes from coast to coast. One of the reasons the lottery has become so popular both in the United States and Canada is that, if by some remote chance one wins, it means a fortune of $140,000, less taxes. The odds against one's ever winning, of course, are astronomical. They have been calculated at something like 450,000 to 1, but some nine million Americans, undeterred, annually invest in $3 Sweepstakes tickets, many of them three times a year.

Why do they do it? It is perhaps a commentary on our times that the popularity of the Irish Sweeps is based, in part at least, upon the same psychology that has made the numbers racket the favorite gamble of the slums. Just as the slum dweller hopes to hit "the numbers" for a pot of gold that will transplant him from the squalor in which he lives to better surroundings, so do many white-collar workers in reasonably well-paying jobs look to the Irish Sweeps as perhaps the only chance they have (however minute that chance may be) to escape from the drudgery and deadly routine in which their lives are molded. They figure that the loss of $3 three times a year is not going to impoverish them, and if lightning ever strikes, they'll be liberated. As one inveterate Sweeps player remarks: "What else have we got to hope for?"

Nurtured by such sentiments and flaunting a holy aura of charity, the Irish Sweeps have captured the fancy of gambling America as has no other gimmick designed to separate the sucker from his dollar. Professional gamblers hail it as a masterpiece of enterprise, and U.S. Postal inspectors, baffled in their efforts to enforce the law, call it "the greatest 'bleeding heart' racket in the world." Americans generally, however, associate the Irish Sweeps with charity, never with rackets, and until recently the great lottery has run without a single sharp glance being cast in its direction. Yet there are some decidedly peculiar angles to this promotion, as the California Attorney General's office made clear in a special report in February, 1960.

One is struck forcibly by a glaring omission in the accounts that the Sweeps themselves furnish of their activities. Nowhere in their published reports do the Sweeps ever spell out the bite that the promoters take out of the colossal millions flowing in from all over the world. In fact, in the Sweeps' own rendering of finances, the promoters disappear like the little men who were never there, and it is made to appear that the huge Irish Sweepstakes pot is divided 75 per cent in cash prizes returned to the winners, 25 per cent to the hospitals of Ireland.

The only breakdown the public is given shows that, in its thirty years of operation, the Irish Sweeps have raised some $500 million. Of this amount, some $350 million has been distributed in prizes; the rest has gone to hospitals and the Red Cross. But these figures tell only part of the story—the part that comes after all promotional "expenses" have been charged off. Just what comes "off the top" before the hospitals of Ireland get theirs is something for which, quite literally, there is no official accounting. Noel C. Browne, Irish Minister of Health, who has personally supervised the distribution of some 30 million pounds to the hospitals and feels quite proud of the Sweepstakes, nevertheless concedes:

"I am not aware of any accounts which show the amounts collected in the different countries in which the Sweep tickets are sold. The Government makes no attempt to supervise the day-to-day running activities of the Hospital Trust [the promotional outfit]. I am not aware of any figures which would show details of expenditures by the Board in its promotional activities, particularly in those countries where the sale of tickets is against the law."

The phenomenal success of the Sweepstakes promotion aroused the curiosity of California Attorney General Stanley Mosk, who in late 1959 tried to determine how much the great lottery takes out of his state and how it succeeds in functioning, illegal as it is, on such an all-encompassing scale. Examining bank drafts sent to Ireland from just one bank, the Bank of America, he found that activity steps up sharply just before the closing date for the Irish Sweeps. In September, 1959, for example, £26,158 sterling and $115,087.36 were sent to Ireland. A spot check showed that a heavy percentage of these remittances were made by Sweepstakes ticket sellers, and Mosk felt convinced that "on an annual basis the take in California dollars runs into the millions."

Trying to learn the *modus operandi* of the Sweeps, the Attorney General uncovered an intricate system.

Ticket sellers, he found, were engaged "in socially accepted occupations with this as their only illegal activity." A few of the sellers at one time lived in Ireland, or have relatives there now, but most had begun as purchasers of tickets, had then decided to become sellers, and had written to Ireland to get on the mailing list for ticket books. The manner in which the books are mailed to the sellers, and in which they in turn mail their ticket stubs to Ireland and get back official receipts, represents an extremely intricate mail smuggling operation, conducted with the kind of finesse that seems to attest to its being highly organized.

Ticket sellers get their books through the mail in unmarked envelopes about three months before the running of each race. "Interestingly enough," the California Attorney General reported, "these envelopes are postmarked in the United States. They never come from Ireland. The most frequent postmarks encountered were those of New York and New Jersey. However, a considerable amount is mailed here in California. All of the sellers with whom we talked denied having knowledge of the person who mailed the tickets to them. . . ."

In returning the ticket stubs, the sellers mail them to a wide variety of private addresses in Ireland (each to a special name and address contained on a slip of paper inserted with his book of tickets)—never to the Hospital Trust. Three to five weeks after he has mailed his money and stubs, the seller gets back from Ireland, in a plain envelope with no return address, receipts to be distributed to ticket purchasers, assuring them that they have not been sold counterfeit chances on the great 450,000-to-1 gamble.

"We do not know what percentage of the money obtained in this promotion actually goes to charity, nor with what result," Attorney General Mosk wrote. "We do not know the income derived from this enterprise by the promoters, but it is reasonable to assume that it would be substantial in an operation as vast as this is. If any accounting is made to the public on the operation of the Sweepstakes, or the charity itself, we are unaware of it. Certainly an accounting would be expected from a genuinely charitable venture."

These findings of the California Attorney General certainly raise questions, not the least of which is the peculiar concentration of Sweepstakes mailings in the New York-New Jersey area, long the hub of one of the strongest underworld organizations in the nation.

The long and well-documented history of America's disastrous experiences with gambling in all its forms is a record that says that gambling is essentially a racket—a falsely alluring "something-for-nothing" business—and that, even under legal auspices, the temptations are such that greedy and grasping hands are almost always stretched out to pick the public's pockets. These are truths, however, that are seldom realized. Despite the score sheet, the persistent misconceptions about the intrinsic nature of gambling and the rackets are appalling.

Perhaps one of the worst of these misconceptions lies in the very implications of the word, gamble. This implies that the bettor has an even chance, or at least a sporting chance. Yet the truth is that, even under the most legal of systems, he has no chance at all. There is always a heavy mathematical edge riding for the track, the house—or the bookie. Even under the perfectly legal pari-mutuel system, a pool of about 15 per cent of all the money bet on each race is taken "off the top" to pay taxes and defray the costs of operation before the odds are figured. In other words, the bettors, as a class, are inevitably 15 per cent poorer with every race that is run. If they are gambling off-track with a bookie, they are about 20 per cent poorer, for the bookie not only pockets the 15 per cent the track takes but he also pays lower odds on long shots. It should be obvious that no habitual and regular bettor can long buck such heavy percentages without going broke.

A series of elaborate studies that show with mathematical precision the inevitable disaster that awaits the bettor has been made by Philip G. Fox, a professor at the University of Wisconsin. After studying gambling odds and percentages for twenty years, Professor Fox wrote in a *Saturday Evening Post* article:

"No one who bets regularly on horses or other sports with bookies, or bucks the house percentages in craps, roulette, and slot machines, has the slightest chance of winning in the long run. The longer he plays, the more staggering are the odds against him. This statement does not apply to card games involving skill and psychological factors. I am discussing only games of chance where the odds are fixed before the action begins—though it might be clearer to say the odds are stacked against the player; he is up against percentages that make it impossible for him to win."

Even if you consistently played the favorite in horse races, you would wind up losing, Professor Fox found. True, about 35 per cent of the favorites win, but they usually pay so little that they cannot possibly overcome that "off the top" bite and the losses of the 65 per cent that fail. Other gambling rackets are even worse. Football pools are almost outright larceny, with the promoters taking, at a minimum, a 53 per cent profit and at a maximum, on widely distributed pools, 92 per cent

Equally horrendous is the beating a player takes on slot machines. The mechanism of the slots can be fixed, and is fixed, to establish a definite percentage of payout. In Las Vegas' more reputable joints, the machines are supposedly set to give the house a steady 6 per cent of all the cash gambled, with the rest being distributed to the players in jackpots; but in more larcenous establishments, it is not unheard of for a machine to be rigged to keep as much as 85 per cent of the money played, leaving a trickle of only 15 per cent to be returned to the "lucky" players.

The general public, however, seems unable to comprehend the meaning of such one-sided odds. It continues to conceive of gambling as a sporting chance—not a sure thing rigged against the bettor. It continues to equate gambling with more innocent games and with private wagers.

"There is great general confusion about the whole problem," says one of the New York Commission of Investigation experts. "People have a tendency to think that their own social gambling is much the same as professional illegal gambling. They don't distinguish between the two, but actually there is all the difference in the world. There is no comparison between a friendly neighborhood poker game and the kind of professional racket in which the sucker doesn't have a chance. If the Vanderbilt stable and the Whitney stable want to run their horses and bet on them, there is no relationship between this gentleman's sport and gentleman's wager, and the activity of a bunch of greedy bastards that are out to defraud the public."

In similar vein, the Massachusetts Crime Commission concluded that the public, which is often blamed for being apathetic, is often not so much apathetic as uninformed. The commission analyzed the returns of six referenda held in Massachusetts to authorize the legalization of pari-mutuels at horse and dog tracks. It found that, despite widespread misconceptions about the nature of gambling, there was always sturdy opposition, and it concluded that "*legalized gambling* exists in Massachusetts by a thin margin." Though racing interests were always highly vocal and efficient in their propaganda, they still failed in many cases to win a clear-cut majority at the polls. In all six dog-racing referenda and in two of the horse-racing tests, pari-mutuels were carried by minority votes; in each case, the real balance of power lay with a sizable segment of the electorate that evidently had not been able to make up its mind and so expressed no preference. From this the Massachusetts commission concluded even legalized racing has far less of an overwhelming mandate than is generally supposed. And the commission added: "It will hardly be suggested that all who voted for legalized gambling were also in favor of unorganized, unlawful gaming and its incidents. It may be wondered what the referenda results would have been if it had been foretold that a big illegal gambling business would go hand in hand with legalized pari-mutuels."

Paradoxically, in the light of such clear findings and such past history, there seems today in many quarters to be a creeping inertia and acceptance that leads to the rationalization that the only way to deal with gambling is to legalize it. Even Justice Murtagh, who cracked down on the policy rackets in New York because their corruption was reaching even into the courtroom, is an exponent of this field of thought. In an article in *The Atlantic Monthly* in November, 1960, he advocated the legalization of off-track betting and questioned "the double standard" that discriminates between a bet at the track and a bet off the track. "The underworld is thriving on our hypocrisy and stupidity," he wrote. "So long as we persist in our efforts to end gambling by prohibitory legislation, we promote police corruption."

This argument seems so beautifully simple that it deceives many otherwise intelligent persons. It seems so easy to say that since gambling is undeniably a racket that has corrupted the law, you can abolish the racket and remove the corruption by making everything legal. But the first probing question usually reveals the incomplete understanding and faulty logic that underlie such proposals. It is elementary to ask, if one is going to legalize bookmaking, just what is one going to legalize? Just horse-race betting? What about baseball? Football? Basketball? Boxing? What about lotteries and the numbers? What, if you will, about slot machines and gambling casinos? If off-track betting is to become legal, where does one draw the line? New York City's proposals have visualized only the legalization of off-track horse-race betting. But this, as the state commission showed, represents only the lesser part of a bookie's illegal business—no more than 42 per cent and probably as little as 30 to 35 per cent. It is folly to suppose that the legalization of one-third of a bookmaker's business is going to make that gentleman foreswear the other two-thirds—and so put an end to all corruption.

The difficulties in which the proponents of legalization often become enmeshed in trying to reduce their program to specifics were illustrated in a friendly debate in the fall of 1960 between Jesse Gordon, public relations man for *The Nation,* in which the first version of this book appeared, and a Democratic district leader in Manhattan. The politician began by stating the favorite thesis of the New York Democratic administration: "We ought to have legalized gambling because gambling can't be stopped, so the government might as well get the revenue instead of the racketeers."

"Well, where would you stop legalized betting?" Gordon wanted to know.

"I would have off-track betting on just the races and prizefights," said the district leader.

"What about baseball? Football? The numbers?"

"No, that would be impractical. We can't bother about all that small stuff. It would be impossible to regulate."

Gordon pointed out that this "small stuff" wasn't really very small, that literally millions of dollars are being wagered on sports, and he suggested that, if the government was going into the business of getting betting revenue, it might just as well get it *all,* instead of leaving juicy hunks for the racketeers.

The district leader became a little flustered at this point, but he stuck doggedly to his thesis.

"It would be impossible to regulate *everything,*" he acknowledged. "But gambling can't be stopped—people want to gamble. Let's recognize it and take it away from the racketeers and get some money to build schools and things."

At this point Gordon carried the politician's argument to its logical limits. "Look," he said, "by government's going into the gambling business, it would be encouraging vice instead of eliminating it or lessening it. On the same principle you are using, it would be just as logical to argue that, because sex is here to stay, the government should be operating whore houses too."

"Whore houses are different," said the district leader sourly.

Such discussions serve to illustrate the illogic underlying arguments for legalization. Experience and common sense dictate that if it becomes legal to make off-track bets on the horses, it is inevitable that this sanction will be used (as the legalization of pari-mutuels has been used) to justify every kind of betting activity. As the Massachusetts commission wrote: "If legalizing of off-track betting on horses or dogs or any other form of gambling product is meant, the advocates must give serious thought not only to the problems arising from opening wider the gates to legalized gambling, but to controlling organized illegal gambling in a more 'wide-open' community."

What emerges from all this is the fact that the American public today is confronted with two clear-cut alternatives, though it is usually told in effect that it has no choice, that it can go in just one direction. It must insist on greater probity in public office, on strict enforcement of current laws which are rooted, not in prejudice, but in the disastrous experience of the past; or it must resign itself to throwing the doors wide open to every kind of gambling and become a society of parasites.

This issue was put in the strongest terms by Governor Thomas E. Dewey in 1950 in a message to the New York Legislature denouncing Mayor O'Dwyer's original off-track proposal. Dewey called the plan to legalize off-track betting "shocking, immoral, and indecent." He continued:

"It is fundamentally immoral to encourage the belief by the people as a whole in gambling as a source of family income. It would be immoral for government to make available to all of its people a state-wide gambling apparatus with the implied assumption that the gains of chance were a fair substitute for or supplement to the honorable business of producing the goods and services by which the people of the nation live.

"It would be an indecent thing for government to finance itself so largely out of the weaknesses of the people which it had deliberately encouraged that a large share of its revenue would come from gambling.

"I recognize that the state and some municipalities now receive a comparatively small revenue from pari-mutuel betting at the tracks. I have always had personal doubts about the wisdom or the morality of this system, but it is confined to those who are actually able to be present at the track and therefore is not a lure dangled before all people in all walks of life and near every home."

Dewey added that, if off-track betting were legalized, "there would be no logic at all" in refusing to legalize every other type of gambling under the sun. "There is no logical place at which the line could be drawn and law enforcement would then break down completely," he wrote.

In conclusion, Dewey cited the record of the past and declared: "The entire history of legalized gambling in this country and abroad shows that it has brought nothing but poverty, crime and corruption, demoralization of moral and ethical standards, and ultimately a lower living standard and misery for all the people."

Anyone who would see these words translated into everyday reality does not have to go to Las Vegas. Though it is not generally realized, Maryland is now one of the major centers of slot-machine activity in the nation. One of the largest manufacturers of one-armed bandits, a transplanted Chicago firm, is the Ace Manufacturing Co., located at Glen Burnie, a suburb of Baltimore. The firm also maintains an assembly plant in Reno and produces 80 to 90 per cent of the slot machines used there; it is also the only legal supplier of machines in four counties of southern Maryland, where legalized slots do a $12-million-a-year business. Maryland machines, according to Arthur D. Laurance, president of Ace, are set at the factory to pay out 80 to 85 per cent. However, the personal experience of players, almost uniformly tragic, would seem to indicate that few machines treat their patrons so generously.

"Of course, we can't control the percentage after a machine leaves the factory," Laurance admits, with a smile. "As a machine gets older it tends to tighten up and decrease the payout."

Or perhaps someone does a little tightening up of the mechanism.

A survey by the Washington *Post* in early 1960 gave a vivid picture of the slot-machine gambling frenzy in Charles County, Maryland. Here garish, neon-lighted roadside gambling houses cluster along a twenty-mile strip of road from Waldorf to the Potomac River Bridge. Some of the larger houses display batteries of more than one hundred slots, and the clang of dropping coins and pulling levers goes on all night.

Women seem to be the most fanatic patrons of the slots. Fistfuls of coins in hand, they stand before the monsters for hours, their hoard of coins vanishing as if dropped into quicksand. One District of Columbia couple told Thomas R. Kendrick, the *Post* reporter, that they played the quarter machines about three nights a week, at a loss of about $20 a night. At 2 A.M. Kendrick found one stocky farm woman still standing before a slot into which she had been pouring coins for five hours. Her five-year-old son tugged at her skirts wanting to go home, but she paid him no attention. One man who said he'd poured $50 into a machine, and so "it's ready," cashed a check for $10, played that too—and found it wasn't. A local electrician turned away broke; he had, he said, fed eighty silver dollars into a slot machine in twenty minutes.

This is hardly the picture of a healthy society. Whether gambling is legal or illegal, it breeds an addiction as destructive of personality, as ruinous to family life, as addiction to liquor or narcotics. It is no coincidence that Alcoholics Anonymous now has its counterpart in Gamblers Anonymous. The need for such an organization is in itself expressive of the illness. There is, as Chief Parker said, no justification for a society that encourages such a disease and "bases its financial structure on the weaknesses of its people."

There not only is no justification, but even when considered from the narrowest and most mercenary standpoint, there is no sense. Can anyone doubt that the American economy would receive a vital shot in the arm if the present $9 billion pocketed annually by the gambling underworld were invested, as most of it otherwise would be, in the purchase of useful goods and services? Even legal on-track betting and legal slot-machine gambling foster crime and deplete the pool of dollars that are left for productive businesses. In Los Angeles, some years ago, veteran policemen contended that the city had about one-tenth the number of bookies, gamblers, confidence men, prostitutes, dope peddlers, touts, and gunmen before Santa Anita opened that it had afterwards. They maintained that even legitimate race tracks, ethically operated, attracted a periphery of riffraff, the inevitable by-product of a something-for-nothing business. At the same time the general manager of one of Los Angeles' largest department stores reported that receipt of bad checks doubled during racing season, that absenteeism increased, that time payments fell off as much as 30 per cent. These complaints from Los

Angeles can be matched item for item in my own state of New Jersey, where merchants maintain they can tell almost to the day the opening date of a racing meet by the nose dive their businesses take.

Extension of legalized gambling means only an extension of these debilitating forces. David Hume, a former trial attorney for the Department of Justice and a resident of Charles County, Maryland, has calculated (*The Nation*, Feb. 13, 1960) that the legalization of slot machines has cost his home county literally millions of dollars in normal growth. Hume recognizes that slot-machine revenue did mean $399,190 to Charles County in 1958, and that this did keep the tax rate to $1.35 compared to a $2 state average and $2.48 in nearby Montgomery County. But he argues that Charles County is as close to Washington as Montgomery, that it has even finer natural advantages, that it should be an ideal residential section for the sprawling capital. As a result of its marriage to gambling, however, the honky-tonk rather than the suburb has become its symbol. It lacks the high-quality developments, the estates, the expansive golf courses such as former President Eisenhower's own Burning Tree that give neighboring Montgomery County its distinction. Hume argues that to get the benefit of approximately $400,000 in gambling revenue the 30,000 residents of Charles County have sacrificed more than $32 million in reduced land values.

None of the arguments so often advanced in support of legalized gambling will stand strong scrutiny in the light of day. Gambling, as the Massachusetts commission so strongly pointed out, is *not* a basic human instinct, but an acquired and cultivated habit that grows with exposure to temptation—with the proximity to race tracks and the stimulus of a current racing season. It is *not* true that there is no difference between a bet inside the track and a bet off the track; there are many and vital differences between the track that provides specific services and offers recreation, and a racket that provides nothing and represents nothing but calculated theft. Equally invalid is the analogy so often used by betting advocates to equate Prohibition with the present ban on gambling. Liquor, as crime commission experts frequently point out, is after all a definite, specific product that produces a known effect. If used in moderation, it may be argued that it has positive values—that it relaxes nerves in moments of stress or internal tension, and serves acceptable social functions. In any event, the purchaser is getting something for his money and knows from experience precisely what he is getting. In betting, on the other hand, he gets nothing; with its immutable percentages always operating against the bettor, gambling in all its forms is, as Professor Fox wrote, nothing more "than a license to steal."

To most rules there are some exceptions; in gambling, one of the most oft-cited exceptions is to be found in the presumed need of resort areas to let down the bars and lure visitors. Even those who recognize the evil of professional gambling sometimes accept the favorite argument of resort interests: "It brings people to town and helps business."

A few years ago Governor LeRoy Collins of Florida chose to question this questionable thesis. Traditionally Florida had been a wide-open state. For years, during the winter, it was the southern home of the nation's most eminent racketeers and the hub of gambling syndicates; it supported some of the nation's most flourishing bookmaking and numbers operations; and illegal casino gambling ran at a multi-million-dollar tempo, virtually with official sanction. Discussing the widely prevalent attitude of the state in a *Saturday Evening Post* article in 1956, Governor Collins wrote:

"There was an attitude in our state for a long time that, to attract the tourists who contribute so vitally to our economy, we had to give them the opportunity to 'live dangerously' and squander their money recklessly. . . . 'Gambling,' some people maintained, 'is entertainment, and tourists ought to have the chance to gamble if they want to.' "

Collins didn't believe this. He felt that tourists who had been suckered out of their last available dollar by professional sharpies would go home with a bad taste in their mouths and no love for Florida. "More than that," he wrote, "a city which condoned gambling exposed its people to the influence of big-time racketeers, and it seemed to me that the moral welfare of our citizens, present and future, was more important than the money the gambling-minded tourists brought in."

Laws were passed outlawing slot machines, and anti-bookie statutes were strengthened. Nobody pretends that Florida suddenly became purified overnight, but the difference that these changes wrought soon became noticeable.

"These actions did not hurt our economy," Governor Collins declared. "In fact, the opposite was true. Daytona Beach showed clearly what effect a gambling crackdown would have on the tourist trade. The year after Daytona Beach closed down gambling it did a much better tourist business than ever before, and it has improved consistently, attracting the kind of people who come as friends, not overnight fortune hunters."

These words clearly put the issue. Either we are to become a society based on solid, worthwhile principles, or we are to become a nation of "overnight fortune hunters" with all the rackets and evil and corruption that this way of life inevitably entails.

9

WHERE DO WE GO?

THE approaching Christmas season in 1942 was shadowed by a tragedy that, even amid the tragedies of war, seemed especially horrible. On the evening of November 28, fire broke out and swept through the Cocoanut Grove, one of Boston's best-known nightclubs. Panic raced the flames, and some 500 persons were smothered, burned, or trampled to death.

Attorney General Robert T. Bushnell, of Massachusetts, probed the causes of the disaster, and the picture that he developed had a significance that endured long after the glaring headlines had faded. The Cocoanut Grove had been built by "King" Solomon. Solomon, with Lucky Luciano and Joe Adonis and a few others of equally eminent rank, had been one of the rulers of the great East Coast bootlegging cartel of late-Prohibition days; he was the most notorious racketeer in Boston, and he dominated all types of rackets. His entire career, up to the time of his murder in 1943, was built upon the systematic bribery of officials and the circumvention of every law.

The Cocoanut Grove, which was owned at the time of the fire by Solomon's attorney, was the perfect example of what happens when the philosophy of the rackets penetrates the field of legitimate business. Recalling the Cocoanut Grove tragedy in an interim report in July, 1955, the Massachusetts Crime Commission wrote:

"The Bushnell investigation established that the nightclub was built and grew on the profits from illegal and criminal business. The owner was found guilty of manslaughter by virtue of wanton and reckless conduct upon evidence showing the absence of fire doors, exits locked, blocked and hidden, inflammable decorations, and estimates of from 1,000 to 1,150 patrons present with capacity for 775. The evidence showed that such overcrowding was not unusual or even the worst instance. The fire was started by the careless holding of a lighted match too close to the inflammable decorations by a sixteen-year-old boy employed in violation of the law.

"The Cocoanut Grove is a tragedy best forgotten for most purposes, but it should never be forgotten for all purposes. For the purposes of this Commission, it demonstrates what Kefauver and others have since demonstrated. The profit motive is the exclusive ruler in the rackets. The greater the profit the greater the risks for the racketeer, but especially for society."

This Boston tragedy was an especially horrible example of the wages reaped by a society that enters into partnership with the mob, an alliance that can only end by making the mob and mob philosophy dominant. It is often said that ever since there has been government, there has been corruption. But there has not always been this *kind* of corruption, and therein lies the difference. This corruption represents an unholy tie between public officials and the leaders of our society on the one hand and the basest elements of that society, the cut-throats and murderers of the underworld, on the other. Joseph Manners, in his testimony before the New York Commission of Investigation, emphasized this.

"Seldom do police or other public officials accept a bribe in murder or rape cases," he said. "Rarely have whole governments been tainted by corruption arising out of crimes of violence. Yet, once corrupted in areas of commercial illegality, the corrupt official must continue his illegal operations with the Syndicate even when it engages in the most vicious underworld violence, such as gang murders or beatings of defaulted debtors."

This partnership of the supposed best and the indisputable worst poses for America one of its deepest and most disturbing problems. It is a partnership that breeds a deep conviction that nothing matters so much as money; that breeds a deep contempt for law; that substitutes for courts of justice the ties of influence; that makes an underworld threat of retribution more persuasive, as demonstrated in the tight-lipped silence of thousands of potential witnesses in murder cases across the land, than any rewards or consideration the law can offer.

The way of the underworld has very nearly become our way of life. It has become so largely through the hypocritical pretense that gambling is an innocent pastime that doesn't really matter. But it certainly matters when a lawyer in upstate New York makes book in the corridors of the courthouse; when a desk lieutenant runs his own book from police headquarters; when Joe Adonis, despite repeated public exposures, can thumb his nose at every law in the state of New Jersey and can enlist the services of local police for his protection; when Carlos Marcello, thoroughly exposed by Kefauver ten years earlier, can wax even richer and be so untouchable in Jefferson Parish that he can reopen a casino supposedly closed by the police; when Tony Accardo, also thoroughtly exposed by Kefauver, can operate his gambling preserves without inhibition; when an unknown Louis Tabet can wander into Las Vegas and can demonstrate that the mere whisper of close acquaintanceship with Dandy Phil Kastel and Jack Dragna serves as a magic passport to the highest circles in Nevada. All of this certainly matters. All of this certainly speaks of a deeply corrupted society that has lost the power to make basic moral distinctions.

What can be done about it? One remedy is obvious—and is in the public's hands. Don't bet—ever—with a bookie. Don't play the slots. Don't patronize professional gambling traps. If these three "don'ts" could ever be translated into action, American gangdom would undergo a swift strangulation. The golden stream that finances bribery and leads to murder would cease to pump through the arteries of the underworld; syndicate crime would die.

This is, of course, a Utopian remedy. The addicted bettor is hardly amenable to reason or any consideration of social ethics. He will seek his thrill, the false promise of something for nothing. As long as such motivations predominate with many bettors, the underworld will retain at least a portion of its customers, but it does not follow that it must retain so huge and so ignorant a clientele. There are doubtless millions of Americans who are not addicted to the daily gamble, who when they bet do so on the spur of the moment and with no understanding of the evil they foster. And there is, of course, another great segment of the public that bets either not at all or very rarely. The free-wheeling style of the underworld can be seriously crimped if these millions of Americans can be made aware of the simple truth—that the two-dollar bettor who patronizes a bookie is not playing an innocent game of tiddledywinks, but is helping to finance the corruption that makes narcotics peddling possible, that makes murder inevitable, that leads in extreme cases, at least, to the actual dominance of the mob over organized society. This is what we buy when we play with the books, and an America that realizes this, that becomes sufficiently aroused and angry about it, can in the end compel reforms.

It is obvious that, serious as corruption is on the local level, the derelictions of the law that matter most are the federal. Syndicated crime, blithely crossing state lines to send a murder squad from New York to perform an execution in California, is decidedly more than a local enforcement problem; it is a national menace with which only federal agencies, having national jurisdiction, can deal. A Tollin operation in Wilmington, the purveying of "the line" from Minneapolis and Chicago, may indeed be operations so finely balanced on the knife-edge of legality that local authorities are frustrated to find an excuse to prosecute; but fitted into the pattern of a national bookmaking conspiracy, it is hard to see how these—or the layoff operations in Biloxi and Covington—could long continue to nurture multi-billion-dollar gambling if federal laws were strictly enforced.

This is precisely the area in which much less has been done than could and should be done. The Federal Bureau of Narcotics and the Internal Revenue Bureau, both agencies of relatively limited scope, have sparked major mob prosecutions from the days of Al Capone to the more recent era of Vito Genovese. Both services, however, are restricted to their own special fields, often are hampered for lack of adequate manpower, and cannot possibly deal with the mighty problem of national crime. The federal agency with the broadest jurisdiction and by far the greatest manpower, the one best situated and equipped to cope with the menace of syndicated crime, is obviously the FBI. This organization and its director, J. Edgar Hoover, have become national idols, and the average American undoubtedly envisages it as the nemesis of the underworld, yet as the record conclusively shows, Hoover and the FBI have never challenged the real overlords of American crime.

Immediately after the repeal of Prohibition, Hoover proclaimed that the big-time gang moguls were switching to kidnaping as a substitute racket. The furor over kidnaping resulted in the passage of new federal laws, the broadening of the FBI's jurisdiction, and numerous well-publicized and successful manhunts. Yet actually, as the history of the last thirty years demonstrates, Hoover's interpretation was quite wide of the mark. Only two-bit bums and desperados turned kidnapers; the Frank Costellos and Meyer Lanskys of the American underworld were many leagues removed from such stupid, risky, and essentially penny-ante crimes. Their real gold mine was gambling—bookmaking, policy, lottery operations, and the gambling casinos, that have poured literally billions of dollars into underworld coffers and corrupted officialdom at every level.

Though it is true that Hoover serves under the jurisdiction of the Attorney General and the Justice Department, his prestige is such that he can hardly be considered a subordinate. Who remembers the names of the Attorney Generals of the past thirty years? Who doesn't know J. Edgar Hoover? The kind of outcry Hoover authored against kidnaping, if directed at the really important rackets of the underworld, could be a force of inestimable good. Such an outcry, however, has not been forthcoming, and even today Hoover's FBI exhibits a curious astigmatism about syndicate crime. Its annual Uniform Crime Report catalogues seven major categories of crime: homicide, forcible rape, robbery, aggravated assault, burglary, larceny, and auto theft. It does not list the really big enterprises of the underworld—the gambling rackets or such syndicate crimes as narcotics smuggling and peddling, with which gambling is so often allied.

This performance represents something less than a call for an all-out crusade against the underworld, and it is stressed here at some length because Hoover's influence, thrown onto the scales, could be of tremendous assistance in the crime-fighting field. Yet Hoover, far from seeking an extension of federal police powers or calling for all-out war on syndicated crime, actually has opposed such moves. In 1952 the National Association of Police Chiefs was considering a resolution recommending the establishment of a national crime commission, but the FBI, according to Police Chief Parker of Los Angeles, secretly fought the proposal and nothing came of it.

In an interview in late December 1960, Parker called attention to Hoover's persistent opposition to the establishment of a new unit or commission in the federal crime-fighting field. Hoover has told Congress, Parker said, that the FBI has all the information that is needed and would supply it to any police department that wasn't corrupt, inefficient, or unable to maintain a confidence. "That could include almost every department in this country," Parker pointed out.

"The FBI shows great interest when stolen property moves across a state line," he continued, "but little interest when some criminals or criminal mobs move from state to state. I strongly believe crime will destroy America if something isn't done and soon."

Asked whether he thought the FBI could handle the crime-busting job, Chief Parker replied succinctly: "They could, but they have shown no indication that they will or that they want to."

Parker's comments followed a new clash between proponents of a national crime-fighting force and Hoover. This came at the convention of the International Association of Police Chiefs in Washington in early October, 1960. Prior to the convention, the association's committee on organized crime had studied the achievements of Wessel's short-lived task force and had issued a report that said:

"The fact remains that while Organized Crime increases, law enforcement remains 'unorganized' insofar as concerted action, effective policies, and planned methods to halt this increase are concerned. It is true that there are rare and salutary instances of effective and successful prosecution against the top leaders of the Mafia and Organized Crime, but there is no continuity of a program to achieve similar successes."

The committee gave a clear indication of where its sympathies lay in the final paragraph of its report. It wrote:

"Surely, there is widespread concern among all law-enforcement agencies about the continuing spread and influence of Organized Crime and all recognize that we must do something more than promise to cooperate with each other. We need more than passive agreement. There must be aggressive and sustained action. In law enforcement we are accustomed to examining and investigating every proposal for advantages and disadvantages, for the possibilities of success or failure. When we witness a method and a procedure that has been uniquely successful in bagging the Mafia, in successfully convicting twenty of the country's organized hoodlums, in obtaining eighteen indictments in actions still pending, and providing evidence for sixty-one possible violations to the Justice and Treasury Department and the Internal Revenue Service, it behooves us to give serious consideration to the continuation of such a law-enforcement task force."

This was like waving a red flag before the bull. J. Edgar Hoover came out charging. He made it clear that he stands foursquare for local and state law enforcement. The man who heads the most powerful police agency the nation has ever nurtured—an agency that has compiled dossiers on the lives of writers who express ideas it dislikes—was horrified that a unified agency to fight syndicated crime might turn into a Gestapo depriving all of us of our liberties. He said:

"The persons who endorse these grandiose schemes have lost sight of some very basic facts. America's compact network of state and local law-enforcement agencies traditionally has been the Nation's first line of defense against crime. Nothing could be more dangerous to our democratic ideals than the establishment of an all-powerful police agency on the Federal scene. The truth of these words is clearly demonstrated in the experience of nations ruled by ruthless tyrants both here in the Western Hemisphere and abroad."

The effect of Hoover's stand can hardly be overestimated. The tremendous prestige that is his, thrown into the balance against the formation of any new agency (which would be a rival, perhaps?), visibly dampened the enthusiasm the police chiefs initially had felt for action which would lift law enforcement, as their committee had reported, out of its present "unorganized" state.

Yet it should be obvious that federal law enforcement cannot forever turn its back on syndicated crime operating on a cross-continental basis; that federal law enforcement cannot remain a jumble of haphazard, limited-jurisdiction agencies. No one derogates the value and importance of law enforcement on the local level. Local law, if it were not so badly corrupted, could clamp down on bookies and policy operators on the street-corner level. However, some of the most obvious clues to top-level operations—"the line," "the layoff," and the dispatch of fast results—lie in the interstate zone of activity that should make them extremely vulnerable to federal attack. It is ridiculous to decree that the transportation of a stolen car across state lines is a federal offense within the jurisdiction of the FBI but that the FBI should have no responsibility when the underworld flies a pair of killers from another state into New York's LaGuardia Airport to knock off Little Augie Pisano.

Not only are important clues to the underworld's gambling gold mine in the hands of federal law, but so is another vital thread—the billions that go into bribery, the "protection money" that buys the mob its official collaborators. The essence of this is simple. Bribery is one of the most difficult crimes to prove—as gangsters told the Massachusetts Crime Commission, "We don't invite witnesses to the payoff"—yet the mountain of cash that is being funneled into the payoff is too huge to be hidden or conveniently explained. Much of it, almost inevitably from the shady, cash nature of the business, goes unreported; and, such is the dominance of apathy and corrupt politics over the law, it remains unreported—and unchecked. It is rare that one gets a glimpse of the magnitude of the loot such as that furnished in 1953 by the aroused federal grand jury in Trenton, investigating Joe Adonis' North Jersey operations. It charged that the U.S. had lost *$1 million in taxes alone* on money paid out for protection; but when the jury tried to probe this noisome scandal, its efforts were blocked by the U.S. Attorney's office, which insisted the jurors could act only on cases prepared and presented to them by Internal Revenue.

This determined discouragement of the grand jury in itself betrays the sensitivity of the area that the jury wanted to probe. It emphasizes a cardinal fact: that the power to straighten out this unconscionable national moral mess lies primarily in the hands of federal law.

The best indication of what might be achieved in this area may be found in the brief record of Milton Wessel's Special Group on Organized Crime. When Attorney General William G. Rogers set up this special task force, he took a step in the right direction. Prior to this, there was literally no agency in the entire nation to serve as a clearing house of information on syndicated crime. The police chief in Los Angeles might have some details about the activities of one unlovely thug, the police in Detroit might have some other smidgins of information. But there was no way either one could know what the other had; there was no agency that bothered to correlate details or fit the pieces together. This is what Wessel calls "the vacuum" of "splintered" law enforcement. It is a horse-and-buggy approach to the streamlined conspiracies of modern gangdom. Wessel went to work to set up a unified crime-fighting task force. He rounded up every scrap of information that could be gathered from every source—from local police departments, state police, district attorneys, crime commissions, and such federal agencies as the Immigration Service, the Internal Revenue Service, the FBI, the Alcohol and Tobacco Tax Division, and, perhaps most important of all, the Federal Bureau of Narcotics. The activity of his unit made possible deportations, prosecutions for income tax evasion, and the conviction on conspiracy charges of twenty Apalachin hoodlums (although this last verdict has since been set aside by the Federal Court of Appeals). Yet Wessel's unit was in existence for only twenty-one months and in action for even less time than that. It was then disbanded.

Wessel himself protests that Rogers and the Justice Department should not be unfairly criticized for what seems the precipitate decapitation of an effective crime-fighting force. He points out that his unit, when it was formed, was designed to be only temporary in nature and that he himself intended to serve only two years before returning to private law practice. Certain hard facts, however, remain. If the system of the last thirty years—the system under which the Justice Department leaves all the knotty problems of syndicate crime to its criminal division and the separate jurisdictions of U.S. Attorneys scattered throughout the nation—had really worked, where would have been the need to create Wessel's group in the first place? What possible justification could there be for abolishing the Special Group after it had been given just twenty-one months to correct the failures of thirty years? Whatever the ostensible reason, the effect was indisputable—to return the problem of syndicated crime to the chaos of disjointed jurisdictions under which the syndicates have always run riot.

A graphic example of the boon this is to the underworld may be found in the report of the Massachusetts Crime Commission. The commission was amazed to find that, when the federal government passed its gambling tax-stamp law after the Kefauver probe, the bookies of Massachusetts shut up shop in panic. *They remained out of business for a solid six weeks!* They did not resume operations until they had received certain vital assurances—that the Bureau of Internal Revenue did not have sufficient manpower to police the law and, as a result, would rely mainly on local police to report gamblers who had failed to purchase their $50 federal tax stamp. The gamblers then rapidly recovered their aplomb and reverted to their customary contempt for the law. The number who even bothered to purchase the federal tax stamp dwindled steadily year by year until it almost reached the vanishing point. To the Massachusetts commission, all this seemed highly significant. The fact that the entire $2 billion-a-year bookie industry in Massachusetts would close down for six weeks at the first hint of federal action seemed to illustrate what might happen if the federal government ever stirred itself to all-out war on top-level rackets.

That it has not stirred itself, but has virtually given the rackets its blessing, is demonstrated by the manner in which other and even more important provisions of the federal gambling tax law have been allowed to lapse. The law provided, not just for the registration and purchase of a $50 tax stamp by bookies, but for the collection of a 10 per cent excise tax on their gross earnings. It also made it unlawful for gamblers to give false statements about their income and its sources. These were provisions designed to strike the mob in the only place that matters to it, the pocketbook; they were important levers placed in the hands of federal law enforcement. All have been practically abandoned. Manners, Wessel's former aide, exploded wrathfully in discussing the issue in testimony before the New York Commission of Investigation. "We . . . have, maybe, $25,000 excise tax coming in," he said. "It's a ridiculous sum." Wessel agrees that never did a multi-billion-dollar illicit business escape more lightly. Under the gambling-franchise tax law, he explains, the bookies would have to keep accurate records available for audit; they could be jailed for falsification or failure to do so. But federal law enforcement has been obstinately blind to opportunity. "The average businessman has to have a record for everything—but not the books," Wessel says.

The need of the moment becomes painfully apparent. A unified and determined drive by federal agencies on the major money rackets of the underworld, against top-level racketeers and the official collaborators without whose aid they couldn't exist, as Peter Hand said, "for twenty minutes," becomes imperative. Various avenues of approach have been suggested. Wessel himself urged that the Justice Department create a permanent Office on Syndicated Crime. He argued that such a unit, dedicated to this one purpose, would serve as a clearing house for information from all over the nation and would weld together and give direction to a campaign to wipe out crime syndicates. Wessel estimated that such a unit could operate efficiently, with about forty lawyers and seventy-five agents, on a budget of less than $1 million a year. His proposal fell into a bottomless void in the Justice Department and was buried without even an echo.

An alternative was suggested in late March, 1960, by the McClellan Committee of the Senate, which found that crime syndicates were extending their sway across the nation and were threatening to dominate the entire economy through their infiltration of labor unions and business enterprises. The Democratic majority on the committee urged the formation of a National Advisory Commission on Interstate Crime, with power to subpoena witnesses and hold hearings. The commission would be a permanent Kefauver Committee, its purpose to keep constant pressure on the mob, to give constant exposure to racket evils, and so to keep dragging out the kind of information that will assist federal agencies to prosecute.

Wessel is opposed to the crime commission idea. "It is a basic principle of law to couple the power to investigate to the duty to prosecute," he says. "I am opposed to a simple exposure objective, and especially on a permanent basis. It is open to far too many abuses."

Few persons with any regard for civil liberties will argue with his stand, but it is perhaps not too much to suggest that the time is overdue for another Kefauver Committee to focus renewed attention upon the continued dominance and immunity of the American underworld. Certainly enough has been shown here to demonstrate that the Kefauver exposé of 1950-51 did not accomplish its objective; it did not end the pernicious influence that gangdom exercises, it did not put a period to the mob's multi-billion-dollar rackets, its crimes of violence, its corruptive influence. Many of the very racketeers whom Kefauver exposed still ride high and conduct their illegal businesses at the exact sites where they ran them ten years ago. No gesture of complete contempt for the law could be more brazen or more emphatic. To permit this situation to endure is unconscionable. A new inquiry, whipped on by all the fervor Kefauver could give it, is desperately needed.

Such an investigation should focus on certain transparently obvious and vital points; on the long-continuing immunity of the exposed lawless and the reasons for it; on bribery as a major crime in modern American society and on the strengthening of laws and penalties to eliminate it; on the failure of federal agencies to utilize the tools they were given by the federal gambling stamp and franchise tax law; on those twilight zones of legality in which flourish such vital interstate services as "the line," "the layoff," the supplying of fast results. Even more than this, it is crucial that any such new Congressional inquiry should concern itself with the creation within the federal government of a permanent prosecution agency charged with the specific task of ferreting out syndicated crime so that the drive against top-level racketeers cannot again languish the instant the headlines fade. In this connection, a new idea advanced by Milton Wessel deserves serious consideration.

Having failed to arouse any enthusiasm for an Office of Syndicated Crime, Wessel proposes that the President appoint a U.S. Attorney-at-Large to take direct charge of the war on syndicated crime. This super-prosecutor would remain under the authority of the Attorney General, but he would have Presidential backing in "a position of stature," as Wessel describes it; his job would be specific and explicit; and the responsibility for the success of the war on top-level crime would be fixed and inescapable. This last consideration is important. In the present shuffle, with various divisions and a gaggle of U.S. Attorneys all sharing in the act, buck-passing becomes easy and blame for failure is virtually impossible to fix. Under Wessel's proposal, the prestige of the Presidency itself and of the crusading prosecutor who might be named the U.S. Attorney-at-Large would be laid directly on the line in the battle against syndicated crime. This perhaps is too much to expect, politics being what it is, but it is doubtful whether any lesser effort can be effective in rooting out the tentacles of corruption that have made crime a major force in our society.

At this writing, it is too early to tell what tack the new Kennedy administration will take on this vital issue. Robert Kennedy, the brother of the President and the new Attorney General, is known to be deeply concerned about the crime problem as a result of his work as counsel for the McClellan Committee. Newspaper stories from the inner circle picture him as eager to tackle not just the problem posed by the long-term immunity of Teamster leader Jimmy Hoffa, but the entire gamut of syndicated crime. It is devoutly to be hoped that such reports are true. For otherwise we shall probably continue to muddle along with the present system of splintered jurisdictions, with its invitation to corruption and to the cynical philosophy, which has become almost a national credo, that "every man has his price." Certainly, under these circumstances, the world we live in is hardly one to inspire us with pride. Its essence perhaps was captured best in these paragraphs of the Massachusetts Crime Commission's report:

"Early in its investigation, the Commission felt that, with gambling so widespread, it could be that there is a gaming operators' side to the story which it would be important to get for a fair understanding of the problem. Since they showed no disposition to state their case for the record, counsel was authorized to talk completely off the record to them. This found them more talkative, and produced the somewhat surprising fact that they don't make a case for themselves. Their philosophy is very enlightening on the subject of conditions which adversely affect law enforcement and the cures. They are living exponents of the theme that those who work for a living are fools. They admit that money rules them and firmly believe that it rules everyone. They say gambling can't operate without protection. They think it is perfectly all right for police to take money for protection, so long as the protection is delivered as contracted for. They believe that the world operates that way and refer to the purchase of licenses, permits, and other such government franchises as illustrations. When confronted with some fundamental propositions, the integrity of the oath of office, they call them 'Boy Scout stuff.'

"Counsel went to lunch one day with one of them who tried to pick up the check. Counsel refused the offer with the remark that while he was with the Crime Commission no one could buy him a cup of coffee. At a later time, the same man asked the Counsel if that remark was meant to imply that a method of payment deferred until after Counsel was no longer with the Commission would be acceptable. The explanation for that misconstruction of an idle remark was in substance a disbelief that anyone would be disinterested in money. It illustrates how deeply imbedded is their philosophy about money; and since they are not fools one must not be a fool either and think that they have no basis for such beliefs."

In this anecdote is capsuled one of the most vital issues of our times. Either all notions of honor are "Boy Scout stuff" to be adhered to only by fools—or they aren't. Much depends on the resolution of that simple issue. For it should be obvious that no sound and democratic society can long endure if its gauge of merit is the size of the payoff.